Fruitful Mom
Filled With The Spirit
Brenda Lee Gines

Faithistry Studios LLC

Edited, designed, and published by **Faithistry Studios LLC**
www.faithistry.com

Printed in the United States of America

ISBN: **979-8-9946358-0-3**

Dedication

To my husband, Jesse, thank you for the quiet sacrifices, the unseen prayers, and for reminding me, even on my hardest days, that this calling of motherhood is sacred, divine work.

To my children, you are my blessings and my legacy. Each of you has shaped me in ways I never expected and drawn me closer to the heart of God. You have each made me a mother in different seasons, and I thank God for you. I pray you grow into who God created you to be and that the seeds planted in your hearts will bloom into lives anchored in Christ.

And to every mother who picks up this book,

May this book be a gentle reminder that you are chosen, you are growing, and you are never alone.

Contents

Purpose & Vision — VII

How to Use This Book — XI

How to Use This Book: Life Group Edition (10 Weeks) — XV

Introduction: Becoming a Fruitful Mom — XXVII

1. LOVE is the Foundation of It All — 1

2. JOY is Finding Light in the Chaos — 15

3. PEACE is Guarding Your Mind and Heart — 27

4. PATIENCE is Trust in Slow Bloom — 39

5. KINDNESS is Love in Motion — 51

6. GOODNESS is Doing What's Right When No One is Looking — 65

7. FAITHFULNESS is Standing Firm When You Feel Faint — 77

8. GENTLENESS is Strength Under Control — 89

9. SELF-CONTROL is the Heart's Guardian — 101

10. Bonus: When Fear & Faith Collide — 113

11. Prayers & Reflections — 131

Acknowledgements — 149

About the Author — 151

Purpose & Vision

Motherhood is sacred ground; holy, stretching, refining, and beautiful. Yet too often, mothers move through their days feeling unseen, overwhelmed, and unsure if they are doing enough or being enough. This book was written to remind every mother that spiritual growth does not happen away from her family, it happens in the heart of her home. Throughout this book, you will notice imagery drawn from the armor of God, not as a teaching on warfare, but as a reminder that spiritual fruit both grows and protects.

Purpose

The purpose of this book is to:

- Guide mothers into a deeper walk with God through the Fruit of the Spirit.

- Transform everyday moments into eternal impact.

- Strengthen the inner life of mothers so they can cultivate Christlike homes.

- Remind every woman that motherhood is ministry, not a pause from purpose, but a profound expression of it.

- Help heal areas where mothers feel they "missed the mark" by offering grace, wisdom, and restoration.

- Equip mothers to parent from God's presence instead of pressure, comparison, or self-reliance.

This book was born not from perfection, but from experience, repentance, revelation, and redemption; the journey of a mother who learned, sometimes painfully, how deeply children need not just our direction, but our spiritual transformation.

Vision

The vision of *The Fruitful Mom* is to:

- Raise mothers who reflect Christ more than culture.

- Build families rooted in love, joy, peace, patience, kindness, goodness, gentleness, faithfulness, and self-control.

- Restore weary hearts and rekindle hope in seasons of exhaustion or regret.

- Encourage mothers to lead with grace, humility, and strength.

- Create homes where the Holy Spirit dwells, peace reigns, and children grow secure in love and truth.

May this book equip you to mother not merely with effort, but with evidence of the Spirit, teaching your children the Gospel not just through words, but through the way you live, love, apologize, correct, and pray.

A Final Blessing

May every mother who turns these pages:

- Feel seen.

- Feel strengthened.

- Feel redeemed.

- And feel invited to bear fruit that lasts generations.

Because God does not expect you to be perfect; He invites you to be planted, nurtured, and transformed. And from that place, fruit will come; fruit your children will eat from, long after your hands are still and your voice echoes not through rooms, but through their hearts.

For Deeper Reflection

You may also enjoy the *Fruitful Mom Journal: Filled with the Spirit — A Guided Journey*, created as a companion resource to help you reflect more deeply on the themes and Scriptures throughout this book. While the journal is not required to benefit from *Fruitful Mom*, it offers additional space for prayer, reflection, personal application, and spiritual growth. It can be used alongside your reading journey or completed afterward as a way to continue cultivating what God has planted in your heart.

How to Use This Book

D ear Momma,

    This book was written for your heart; the tired parts, the tender parts, the hopeful parts, and the parts still healing. It is not a book to rush through, but one to walk with. Each chapter represents a Fruit of the Spirit, and like fruit in nature, these virtues take time, nourishment, and grace to grow.

This book is not here to tell you to be perfect.

It is here to help you pursue presence, faithfulness, and Spirit-led growth, one day at a time.

You can read this book:

- one fruit at a time per day,

- or once a week for 9-10 weeks,

- or all at once.

There is no wrong pace. Healing and growth are not measured by speed, but by temperance.

As you read, allow the Holy Spirit to speak, convict, comfort, and guide. Let each fruit soften your heart, strengthen your spirit, and realign your motherhood with Heaven's rhythm.

At the end of each chapter, you will find **reflection questions**. Use them prayerfully.

You may:

- journal your responses,

- pray through them quietly,

- or discuss them with another mother or your spouse.

These questions are not meant to expose your flaws but to gently reveal God's hand and His hope in your story.

A Gentle Note for Mothers at Different Seasons

Some chapters may stir memories; moments where you wish you would have mothered differently, spoken gentler, hugged longer, or prayed sooner.

If that happens, pause. Breathe. Invite God's grace into those spaces. He is the God of Restoration.

This book welcomes mothers of newborns, toddlers, teens, adult children, and those rebuilding broken bridges.

God does not expect mothers to never miss the mark; He expects commitment, surrender, and willingness to grow (Philippians 1:6).

Every effort toward Christlike mothering, no matter how small, has eternal weight.

What This Book Is

- A companion

- A gentle guide

- A mirror of grace

- A reminder of who you are in Christ

What This Book Is Not

- A checklist to perform

- A comparison tool

- A measure of "good enough" mothering

- A demand for perfection

Motherhood is a heart posture, not a competition. It is not measured in flawless days but in faithful ones. Before you begin each chapter, take a moment to:

- Meditate on God's presence in your life,

- Whisper a simple prayer: *"Holy Spirit, help me grow today,"*

- Release yesterday's failures, and

- Open your heart to God's voice.

He promises to meet you in the quiet. He delights in your desire to grow. Even if you come to these pages weary, dry, or unsure; you are not behind. You are exactly where He begins new things.

Bonus Chapter 10 Reading

You may notice a bonus chapter titled *When Faith and Fear Collide* later in this book.

This chapter is not meant to be read on a schedule or out of obligation. It exists for moments when growth feels hard, faith feels stretched, or fear feels louder than usual.

If you encounter such a season, this chapter is here for you. If you do not need it right now, you may return to it later or not at all.

Growth is not linear, and God meets you exactly where you are.

As you read, remember:

Fruit grows slowly. Roots develop in hidden soil. And God is patient with you. You are not expected to bear all fruit perfectly... only to walk with the One who grows it within you. May this book become a soft place for your heart to land, a gentle teacher, a healing companion, and a holy invitation to grow into the mother God designed you to be. You are seen. You are loved. You are becoming fruitful, and Heaven celebrates your yes.

With grace and sisterhood,

Brenda

How to Use This Book: Life Group Edition (10 Weeks)

The Fruitful Mom is more than a devotional; it's a journey of spiritual formation for mothers who desire to grow in the character of Christ. Whether this book is used in a church setting, a home gathering, or a small group of friends, these next ten weeks will guide you through practical, Spirit-led transformation.

This guide will help leaders and participants understand what to expect, how to prepare, and how to make each meeting meaningful, relational, and rooted in God's Word.

Life Group Etiquette (For Everyone)

- Grace over perfection — some weeks will feel easier than others.

- Honesty over performance — growth happens in truth.

- Listening over fixing — we don't correct each other; we companion each other.

- Confidentiality over curiosity — what's shared stays here.

Remember to Remind the Group:

"No one is expected to master the fruits—only to walk with the Spirit."

A Note About the Bonus Chapter (Chapter 10)

When Faith and Fear Collide is a bonus chapter written to support mothers during moments when spiritual growth feels difficult, resisted, or emotionally heavy.

As women grow in the Fruit of the Spirit, it is not uncommon for fear, doubt, exhaustion, or spiritual resistance to surface. These moments do not indicate failure; they often signal transition, refinement, and deeper dependence on God.

This chapter is intentionally set apart from the nine fruits. It is **not a tenth fruit**, nor is it required to complete the Fruit of the Spirit journey.

Instead, Chapter 10 serves as a **pastoral companion**—offering reassurance, biblical grounding, and gentle guidance when faith and fear feel intertwined.

Leaders and readers are encouraged to approach this chapter prayerfully and flexibly, using it as needed rather than by schedule.

Life Group Leader Options for Chapter 10

Every group is unique. Leaders are invited to choose the approach that best serves the spiritual and emotional needs of their mothers.

Option A — Personal Reading Only (Recommended Default)

Chapter 10 may be offered as **optional personal reading** for individual reflection.

Use this option when:

- A participant is experiencing anxiety, burnout, or discouragement.

- A week feels emotionally heavy.

- Spiritual resistance is surfacing privately rather than corporately.

How to introduce it to the group:

"If this week stirred fear, weariness, or doubt, Chapter 10 is available as a personal encouragement. Read it only if you feel led." No group discussion is required.

Option B — Optional Group Discussion (Leader-Discerned)

Chapter 10 may be used as a **group discussion** only if the leader senses it would be helpful and appropriate. Leaders may conclude the discussion early if prayer becomes the primary need.

Use this option when:

- Multiple mothers are expressing fear, spiritual resistance, or discouragement.

- The group needs reassurance rather than instruction.

- Prayer and reflection are more needed than structured teaching.

Guidelines for group use:

Select **1–2 reflection questions only.**

- Keep discussion grounded in Scripture and hope.

- Avoid problem-solving or comparison.

- Allow prayer to lead the space.

This chapter should **never replace** a fruit-focused week and should not be rushed or forced.

Weekly struture can be altered to fit your groups needs. Use discernment and follow the promptings of the Holy Spirit. His leading should be your primary focus over any suggested structure provided.

Week 1 — Introduction & Orientation

The first week is all about setting the tone, creating safety, and laying a spiritual foundation.

Purpose of Week 1

- Explain the heart behind the devotional.

- Introducing the Fruits of the Spirit.

- Build community and expectations.

- Create a shared commitment to spiritual growth.

- Establish a group rhythm that will last 10 weeks.

What the Leader May Do Before Week 1

- Read the Introduction and first fruit chapter in advance.

- Pray over each woman in the group.

- Share the weekly structure (below).

- Prepare a welcoming environment: soft worship music, tea/coffee, pens, and optional journals.

Week 1 Meeting Flow

1. **Welcome & Icebreaker** (10 minutes)

A simple prompt: "What brought you here? What fruit do you most desire God to grow in your life this season?"

2. **Group Purpose** (10 minutes)

Share the intention of this study:

- to grow spiritually

- to support one another

- to invite the Holy Spirit to bear fruit in everyday motherhood

- to walk authentically, without pressure or perfectionism

3. **What to Expect** (10 minutes)

- Weekly personal reading

- Reflection questions

- Group discussion

- Prayer and encouragement

4. **How the Book Works** (10 minutes)

- Main Teaching Section

(Blends reflection, lesson, life application, stories, and Scripture)

- Closing Reflection

(A brief summary or meditation that closes the chapter)

- Moments of Reflection

(Reflection questions to discuss)

- Prayer for the Fruit

(An end-of-chapter prayer)

5. Group Expectations & Covenant (5 minutes)

Encourage:

- confidentiality

- kindness

- punctuality

- grace for messy days

- no comparing or discouraging one another.

6. Overview of the Fruits of the Spirit (Gal. 5:22–23) (10 min)

"But the fruit of the Spirit is love, joy, peace, forbearance (patience), *kindness, goodness, faithfulness, gentleness and self-control. Against such things there is no law."*
(NIV)

Share a brief vision of what the next 9 weeks will build.

7. Prayer & Blessing (5 min)

Weeks 2–10 — Weekly Group Rhythm

Each week focuses on one fruit, following a simple, repeatable structure.

Before Each Meeting

Participants should:

- Read the corresponding chapter.

- Complete any reflection spaces.

- Jot down anything the Holy Spirit revealed.

Leader's Guide for Weekly Meetings (60–75 minutes)

1. Welcome & Quick Check-In (5 minutes)

Prompt each mother with:

"How did living this week's fruit show up in your home?"

This keeps the focus experiential, not performative.

2. Scripture Reading (3 minutes)

Read the main scripture(s) referenced in the chapter.

This anchors the meeting in the Word.

3. Chapter Recap (5 minutes)

The leader or a chosen participant summarizes the key takeaway of the fruit.

4. Guided Discussion (20–25 minutes)

Use 3–4 questions like:

- What part of the chapter stood out to you most?

- Where did you struggle to apply this fruit this week?

- What did the Holy Spirit reveal to you about yourself, your home, or your motherhood?

- Did you notice any change in your tone, patience, or reactions this week?

Leader guardrails

Gently redirect conversation if it becomes:

- overly self-critical

- venting without reflection

- focused on fixing instead of supporting

- emotionally heavy without hope

5. Weekly Practice/Challenge Debrief (10 minutes)

Discuss:

- How did the chapter's principles show up in real life?

- What was unexpectedly difficult or easy to follow?

- What small victory did you experience, if any?

- Where did God meet you this week?

6. Prayer Moment (10 minutes)

Encourage a different mother to pray each week.

Inspire prayers that are:

- specific

- supportive

- Spirit-led

- connected to the week's fruit

Option: the leader may read the chapter's closing prayer aloud as a group prayer.

7. Next Week's Fruit Preview (2 minutes)

Briefly share the theme of the next fruit so mothers can begin reading and preparing their hearts.

Leader Tips for a Healthy Group

1. Keep group focus on Scripture, not opinions.

Use scripture and the book as the anchor. You may use other scriptures prompted by the Holy Spirit.

2. Make space for quiet members.

Ask direct but gentle invitations:

"Would you like to add anything?"

3. Protect the room from judgment.

Redirect conversations that drift into:

- Shame

- Criticism

- Comparing children

4. Celebrate small victories.

The Holy Spirit often works in baby steps, not giant leaps.

5. Know when a moment needs prayer over discussion.

If someone is emotional, pause, pray, and point out their strength within their vulnerability.

End of Week 10 — Group Celebration

The final gathering may also include:

- Encouragement for each woman to share one major shift God made in her heart.

- Reading Galatians 5:22–23 aloud together.

- Praying a blessing over each participating mother.

End by reminding the group: "The fruit God grows in you will continue to flourish far beyond these ten weeks."

Introduction: Becoming a Fruitful Mom

Motherhood is one of the most vital callings in existence today. It is also often considered to be one of the most underappreciated and overlooked callings in ministry. Modern society has slowly diminished its value, expecting both mother and father to produce monetary income for the family. As a result, mothers are more exhausted and less prepared to care for and raise their children.

The shift has been subtle, but its effects run deep. What once was honored as a sacred, God-given responsibility is now treated as an accessory to "real" success.

Cultural pressure pushes mothers to pour themselves out everywhere, work, home, relationships, and responsibilities, while rarely giving them space to pour back into themselves or their walk with God.

Homes run faster than ever, but often with less connection. Children have more stimulation, yet less guidance. Families have more conveniences, but less closeness. And mothers, stretched thin between countless expectations, quietly carry a weight the world rarely acknowledges that shapes hearts, builds character, and forms the spiritual foundations of future generations.

Yet despite society's shifting values, God has not changed His mind about motherhood.

It remains a divine calling, a ministry that shapes eternity, a place where discipleship begins long before a child can speak. While the world may overlook the significance of a mother's daily sacrifices, heaven counts every one of them.

Mothers are not failing; they are fighting a cultural current that constantly pulls against their calling.

And in that struggle, God meets them. He strengthens them. He equips them. He reminds them that the work they do whether seen or unseen, is irreplaceable in the kingdom of God.

Because when a mother stands firm in her purpose, she strengthens her home. And when homes are strengthened, generations are transformed.

Motherhood is the place where joy and exhaustion often meet, where love grows deeper through both laughter and tears. Every mom longs to be patient, gentle, and strong, yet finds herself humbled by the daily reality of life. But here's the truth: you don't have to be a self-reliant, perfect mother to be a fruitful one.

God never asked you to parent without His help.

He invited you to parent with His Spirit.

The fruits of the Spirit (love, joy, peace, patience, kindness, goodness, faithfulness, gentleness, and self-control) are not just virtues to admire. They are living qualities that take root in your heart when God's presence shapes your responses, softens your tone, and strengthens your resolve.

This book is an invitation to grow.

To slow down.

To see motherhood not as a list of tasks, but as a garden, a place where God is cultivating both you and your children.

Here you will find real stories, biblical encouragement, emotional clarity, and reflections designed to help you walk through each Fruit of the Spirit with grace and intention.

Some days you will get it right; other days you won't. But God turns even your weakest moments into opportunities for growth.

Every prayer, every hug, every tear, every whispered "Lord, help me" becomes a seed planted in love.

So, breathe, dear mom. You are not behind.

You are becoming.

And with each step, you are growing into the woman and mother God designed you to be... fruitful, faithful, and full of grace.

You don't have to change your whole life to grow fruit.

God will grow it in you right where you are.

"This is to my Father's glory, that you bear much fruit, showing yourselves to be my disciples."

—John 15:8 (NIV)

Chapter One
LOVE is the Foundation of It All

Love is patient and kind,
Love does not envy or boast,
it is not arrogant or rude...
Love bears all things, believes
all things, hopes all things,
endures all things.

1 Corinthians 18:1-7

Love Begins in the Unseen

The love of a mother for her child is unlike anything else on earth. It begins quietly, in the unseen, before the first cry and before the first flickers of a heartbeat on a monitor.

It begins at conception, in the dark quiet place where God ignites the spark of life.

And with that spark comes a divine assignment; one heaven ordains long before the world takes notice. God begins shaping a mother's heart just as He forms the child within her.

Even before a mother sees the tiny face she's been dreaming of, she loves her child. Some may not know how to express it or even how to comprehend it, but beneath every layer of confusion and fear, there is love.

That love may be tested by morning sickness, sleepless nights, and aching uncertainty, yet it grows with every flutter and kick.

It marks the end of self-centered love and the beginning of selfless love. It is a love that gives, protects, and endures.

It is a sacred connection that deepens through both discomfort and awe. It changes not only her body and emotions but also the way she sees the world: through new eyes of protection, compassion, and purpose.

A Sacred Partnership Between Heaven and Earth

Each passing day becomes a partnership between what is visible and what is felt.

The mother provides nourishment, warmth, and shelter, while God shapes every detail within her womb: the heartbeat, the fingerprints, the purpose.

This shared creation becomes a sacred duet between heaven and earth, between divine design and human devotion.

It is a silent bond between Creator and creation. A beautiful parallel that mothers uniquely experience as they feel the unseen movements of the child within them.

She is privileged to form a connection first, after God Himself, with the life growing beneath her heart. This is the blossoming place of love and devotion.

This love is Agape in its purest human form: unconditional and sacrificial, born from the heart of one who gives life. It mirrors the way God loves us, though His love reaches even deeper still.

As Psalm 139:13 reminds us, *"For You created my inmost being; You knit me together in my mother's womb." (NIV)*

What a mystery, that the same God who knits us together also gives us the capacity to love the children He entrusts to our care.

Love Renewed, Love Returned

When a mother finally holds her child for the first time, she experiences the impossible: a love that somehow expands beyond measure.

The baby who moments ago was a part of her womb, is now resting safely against her chest, wrapped in warmth and belonging.

In that moment, both hearts relearn what it means to love one another and to be loved. It is renewed, but somehow transcendent.

This moment of reunion also becomes a reflection of God's own heart; the way His love draws us close even after seasons of separation.

Just as the child recognizes the familiar rhythm of his mother's heartbeat, we too recognize the steady heartbeat of God when we return to Him. Love always brings us back home.

Choose Love Daily

This love does not end with that first embrace.

It is a choice a mother keeps making. Her love begins as instinct, but walking in love each day becomes an act of the will.

She must decide to *"put on love"* (Colossians 3:14) even when it is hard, choosing patience over irritation, grace over guilt, and compassion over control.

There will be days when her love feels unappreciated, days when weariness tempts her to withdraw, and days when she questions whether she is enough.

But love, God's love, does not give up. It endures not because it is easy, but because it is eternal.

Because love is God Himself.

Armored with Love

Love is protected by righteousness, and righteousness is formed by love.

That is why the breastplate guards the heart, the center of all affection, motive, and intention. It protects the place where love begins, where wounds settle, and where a mother's deepest convictions are formed.

When a Fruitful Mom chooses love, she is choosing more than a feeling, she is choosing to shield her heart from bitterness, resentment, and emotional erosion. Choosing love becomes an act of war against every force that tries to harden her spirit.

The breastplate becomes her reminder that true righteousness is not cold perfection, but love lived with purity and integrity, even when life feels overwhelming.

This armor guards her from the slow drift towards hardness and cynicism that try to implant thoughts of, "Why try? Is this worth it?" or sorrow that tempts her to completely withdraw.

With the Breastplate of Righteousness in place, love becomes her strength, not her strain.

Instead of reacting out of hurt, she responds out of wholeness. Instead of protecting herself through distance, she protects her home through love. It guards her for God's purpose.

With every act of love, she reinforces her armor. With every step of obedience, she strengthens its hold. With every surrender to God, she polishes what protects her most.

Because where love is fortified, peace finds its footing, patience grows easier, kindness flows more naturally, and every other fruit begins to flourish.

Love That Endures Every Season

Love is the bittersweet beauty of watching a child grow.

It is rejoicing in every milestone yet grieving quietly as each birthday brings a little more independence, a reminder that her child is becoming someone new.

Motherhood may feel like a wild, unpredictable roller coaster full of dips, turns, and unsteady moments, but love is the unbreakable track beneath her feet. Those tracks of love are steady, sure, and strong.

A mother's love will always be her foundation in every season, just as God's love for us remains the unshakable foundation in every breath we take.

In Galatians 5:22, love is the first Fruit of the Spirit listed. That is because love is the soil where all other fruits grow.

When love takes root, joy, peace, patience, and every other virtue begins to bloom.

Love in Many Forms

C. S. Lewis, in his book **The Four Loves**, described love as coming in many forms: affection, friendship, romantic passion, and divine charity.

As mothers, we experience glimpses of all four every day: the giggle of a child, a friend's encouragement, a partner's embrace, and in God's unconditional love poured into us.

When mothers pause long enough to recognize how God's love surrounds us, gratitude begins to bloom. This gratitude tills the soil of our hearts so that love can grow stronger. It shifts our focus from what we lack to the abundance already around us.

Love then becomes more visible when a mother uses gratitude as a lens.

Through gratitude, God's love then becomes clearer as the revelation of His constant presence becomes rooted in understanding, making it easier to allow His love to flow over your children and spouse.

The Fruitful Mom discovers how to love faithfully as she mirrors God's heart.

Love in Forgiveness

Love is also the place where forgiveness begins.

There will be moments in motherhood when words come out sharper than intended or when weariness overshadows warmth, but even then, her love for her children and their love for her, restores what was broken or injured.

Love reminds a Fruitful Mom that mishaps occur and to not keep tally of anger or pain. Her willingness to release offenses gives her children a living example of how to do the same in their own lives when the time comes.

With every act of love, whether whispered in prayer over a sleeping child, spoken softly after an apology, or shown in simple daily care, is a seed planted within the heart of a child.

Love is an Inheritance

The Fruitful Mom comes to realize that her love carries generational weight.

The tenderness she shows today becomes the compassion her children will remember and offer tomorrow to their own children.

When love becomes the foundation of life, everything else aligns. Peace comes easier, joy shines brighter, and patience becomes possible.

Her home begins to feel like a reflection of heaven, because it is filled with His presence.

And so, a Fruitful Mom keeps choosing love, not as a feeling but as a gift from God that she can pass onto her children.

"Do everything in love." 1 Corinthians 16:14 (NIV)

When Love Feels Lost

There will be seasons when love feels buried. Not gone... but hidden under the weight of life.

Maybe you had a day when your heart felt tired, the kind of tiredness that shows up quietly in the way your voice shakes, or in how long you linger in the bathroom just to breathe.

Maybe you have stood at the sink with tears rising for reasons you cannot fully explain, wondering why love feels harder today than it did yesterday. These are the moments no one sees, yet they shape the deepest places of a mother's life.

A lot of times, days can blur into tasks, and her hands, once lifted in prayer, are now busy holding herself together. She may find herself short-tempered, weary, or withdrawn.

Her reflection can start echoing the strains of surviving life instead of mirroring God's strength.

A mother may even wonder, "Where did my self-love go?" or "Why don't I care about myself anymore?"

The truth is, the love she had for herself never disappeared. It became misplaced.

It hid beneath the piles of laundry, in exhaustion, in frustration, disappointment, and fear.

And it hides behind the pain of being misunderstood or in the realization mistakes were made on her part. It can sometimes hide behind the false belief that you'll have time later to express your affection.

But God has a way of reawakening love, the moment His hands touch it.

Growing in Renewed Love

Getting back on track begins with grace, not guilt.

God does not expect mothers to never miss the mark. He expects mothers to learn from their mistakes and grow in Christ each day.

Making a conscious effort to remember putting God first, and Who He gave in love for her, will help put a mother's love into perspective.

Mothers will begin to understand that God's love will fill the gaps where they feel weak. His mercy will become the reset button for their hearts.

The Fruitful Mom learns renewal comes from identity, not intensity. It comes from resting in God's love.

When a mother gives God her burdens, love begins to bloom again. It begins to light not just her home, but her heart.

And from that steady glow, something else begins to rise... **joy**.

Closing Reflection

Pause and remember: every act of love you give, seen or unseen, plants something eternal in your child's heart.

Personal Insight

There was a season in my motherhood where I believed love meant always being strong, always being composed, and always having the right answer. But God gently revealed that love isn't proven in perfectionism; it is proven in presence.

Some of my greatest moments of loving my children were not the "big" memories, but the subtle ones: sitting beside them when they were afraid, listening when they were frustrated, and praying when I didn't know what to say. Love isn't about fixing everything. It's about being faithful enough to stay, even when you feel weak. In those moments, God reminds me that His love sustains not only my children, but also my own heart.

Moments of Reflection

1. How have you experienced God's love in motherhood: both in the beauty and in the struggle?

2. What would it look like to "put on love" more intentionally this week?

3. How can you remind yourself that love isn't lost when life feels heavy, it's simply waiting to be remembered?

4. In what areas of your daily life do you feel God inviting you to love more deeply, whether through patience, forgiveness, or compassion?

5. What truth about God's love do you need to hold onto in this season, and how can you remind yourself of it when motherhood feels heavy?

Prayer for Love

Father,

Thank You for entrusting me with the sacred gift of motherhood.

Fill my heart daily with Your unfailing love so it overflows into every word I speak and every action I take.

When I feel weary, remind me that Your strength carries me. When frustration rises, help me soften my tone with grace. When I am tempted to withdraw, draw me closer to You and back to my children with tenderness and patience.

Teach me to love not only in emotion, but in action, faithfully, sacrificially, and joyfully.

Help me remember that even on the hard days, I am not alone and that I am worthy of your love. Help me not forget that Your love is the foundation beneath my feet and the power within my heart.

Make my home a reflection of Your presence and let love, Your love, be the legacy I leave in my children.

In Jesus' name,

Amen.

Chapter Two
JOY is Finding Light in the Chaos

*Do not grieve,
for the joy of the Lord
is your Strength.*
Nehemiah 8:10

Joy in the Ordinary

The joy of a mother's heart is not only found in the behavior of her children or her actions alone, but in her presence and representation as a woman of God. It is present in everyday trivialities and mundane routines that run on autopilot.

It lives in between the moments that often go unnoticed, in the ruckus of play, in unexpected circumstances, in the small hand that reaches for hers when craving privacy, and in the quiet exhale at the end of the day.

Joy can be hidden in the screams of shouting siblings on a tired morning. It can be tucked between slammed doors and scattered toys. It could be lost in a messy closet that was once clean.

Joy is the light that keeps glowing, reminding you that happiness may fade, but joy endures.

This is because God's joy is always present on every occasion.

It is not a fleeting emotion that gets carried off by every blowing wind that passes by. It is firm and never-ending.

Mothers simply need to become more mindful of what perspective they choose to view life with, when they're busy or tired. Joy shifts when perspectives change.

Choosing Joy Daily

For many mothers, joy is something that feels just out of reach.

Maybe you've had mornings when you woke up already feeling behind, when the weight of yesterday slid into today before you even had a chance to breathe. Maybe you've stood in a quiet kitchen with your hands on the counter, staring at nothing, wondering why joy feels distant even though you love your family deeply.

The demands of life, the exhaustion, and the disappointments all press hard against the heart and can drain the energy in your day.

Those private moments, the ones where your smile feels tired and your heart feels overburdened, are the moments that make joy feel so far away. And yet, they are also the very places where God is closest.

Joy is something a mother learns to "put on," by looking at the world through renewed eyes. It was never meant to be chased. It was meant to be chosen.

Just as love opens the doors to gratitude, joy enables you to walk through them, helping reveal all the blessings that surround you.

If you pause long enough to recognize the trivial things, you will suddenly realize you're more blessed than you believed. And when you choose joy, you begin to appreciate all that you have.

Changing your mindset does not change the circumstances you're living in, but it does change the perception and attitude you carry each day.

The Helmet of Joy

Joy doesn't just uplift a mother's emotions, it protects them. That is why joy pairs with the Helmet of Salvation. A helmet guards the head, and in the same way, joy guards the mind. It keeps her thoughts anchored in truth rather than tossed by circumstances.

The enemy often attacks a mother first in her thoughts:

"You're failing."

"Everyone else is doing life better than you."

But the Helmet of Salvation interrupts those lies with identity:

"You are redeemed."

"You are chosen."

"You are His."

This helmet protects a mother's mind from spiraling thoughts and hopeless patterns of constant comparison, overthinking, and imagined fears.

It reminds her that she is saved, secure, and held by God, no matter what motherhood throws at her. When her thoughts drift towards negative thinking, the helmet redirects her gaze to Christ's victory.

Joy becomes a mindset, not a mood. It steadies her thinking, strengthens her perspective, and shields her from the mental battles that try to steal her joy.

Joy is not the absence of turmoil. It is the calm within it. Like the stillness in the eye of the storm. It is living and experiencing life the way God intended, even when gray skies clutter the view.

The Fruitful Mom learns that joy is not merely felt, it is worn.

When Joy Doesn't Feel Consistent

If you ever reach a moment when you don't feel consistent joy with your children, do not mistake that feeling for failure or become ashamed. Your children still find joy in you, even through any emotions that can temporarily cover it up.

They see it in the safety of your presence, in the comfort of your voice, and in the consistency of your care. Even in those times you may feel empty... they are being filled.

In time, what they reflect becomes your reminder that joy never truly left.

It had spread and multiplied through them.

Doubling Joy

This multiplication of joy is conducted between mother and child, through the passing of time. It is nurtured through encouragement, forgiveness, and companionship.

The smile of a mother, her laughter, and her faith in the middle of troubles become the pillars of strength and the foundation of enduring memories that adult children would want to pass on.

Joy Beyond Circumstance

Over time, the Fruitful Mom sees that joy is not something the world can give or take. It is born of divine perspective.

It is the ability to see light even in shadow, to find laughter after tears, and to rest in knowing that every moment, no matter how messy, is sacred when surrendered to God.

Joy is more than a smile; it's a power that bubbles up when you may have already run dry. It is the inner light that refuses to be dimmed by trials.

You might not always feel happy, but joy doesn't depend on your feelings or what you have or don't have.

It depends on appreciation.

It's what keeps your soul steady when your emotions sway. Happiness can be shaken by what happens, but joy stands because of Who stands with you.

Redefining "Enough"

Joy also redefines what "enough" means.

It teaches a mother that even when the house isn't spotless, the plan isn't completed, or the day ends unfinished, she can still be full.

Not out of her own works, but from her understanding of God and how He works. His joy fills the spaces that performance never could. The Fruitful Mom understands that God fills every place, even those that are neglected due to circumstance.

Life Through Joy

When choosing to live life through the eyes of joy, everything looks brighter.

The interruptions become invitations. The noise becomes music. Joy turns those unbearable moments into learning experiences and appreciation.

Even so, fatigue can descend upon a mother unexpectedly.

The Fruitful Mom identifies this fatigue as the byproduct of her love being poured out onto good ground, her children.

A Prayer for Joy

So, when life feels too loud, too heavy, or too uncertain, whisper this prayer:

"Lord, help me find Your joy again. Teach me to see light where I only see clutter, peace where I only feel pressure, and beauty where I only notice burden."

Because joy doesn't come from having a perfect life. It comes from walking daily with a perfect God who never leaves.

When you let joy take root, it begins to calm what once felt restless. The laughter that once filled your home now settles quietly into gratitude. And from that gratitude, something steady begins to rise... **peace**.

"You make known to me the path of life; you will fill me with joy in your presence."

Psalm 16:11 (NIV)

Closing Reflection

Take a slow breath and look for one small moment of joy today... God is willing to direct you to it. Are you willing to acknowledge it?

Personal Insight

I used to think joy depended on circumstances feeling peaceful, orderly, and predictable. But motherhood rarely looks like that. Joy has surprised me in the messy places; in the laughter after tears, the silly conversations at the dinner table, and in the joy that rises after prayer when nothing around me has changed but something inside me has.

God has taught me that joy isn't a mood; it is a posture of the soul. It is remembering that even in exhaustion, uncertainty, and daily routines, His presence is my strength. Joy doesn't deny difficulty. It declares that God is with me in it and that I have access to His joy because I belong to Him.

Moments of Reflection

1. When was the last time you felt pure joy, and what happened at that moment?

2. How do you usually respond when joy feels far away? How might God be inviting you to find it differently?

3. Have you mistaken busyness for fruitfulness? How could slowing down make more room for joy?

4. In what ways has gratitude helped you uncover joy in your daily life?

5. How might your children experience joy through you, even on days when you don't feel it yourself?

Prayer for Joy

Father,

Thank You for the gift of joy; joy that is not fragile like emotion but anchored in Your unchanging presence.

On days when noise overwhelms me and my heart feels tired, remind me that joy is not lost; it is waiting to be seen again.

Teach me to pause and notice Your goodness in the simple moments, the laughter, the stillness, the small mercies that whisper Your love. Help me choose gratitude over grumbling and presence over hurry.

When heaviness settles in and joy feels far away, lift my eyes back to You, the Source of every good and perfect gift. Let Your joy strengthen me, steady me, and spill over onto my children so they learn what it means to find light even in life's disorder.

Fill my home with laughter, my heart with peace, and my days with Your presence.

In Jesus' name,

Amen.

Chapter Three
PEACE is Guarding Your Mind and Heart

Peace I leave with you,
My peace I give to you...
Let not your hearts be troubled,
Neither let them be afraid.

John 14:27

Silence... is Peace

Take a moment to imagine closing your eyes as you lay back on a comfortable seat or couch, resting your head on a cozy pillow.

You find yourself finally relaxing in the quiet sensation of comfort and immense peace from the stillness of your home. For the first time, in a long time, you recall what it feels like to be alone.

You sip your coffee, tea, or water and savor the silence, because for whatever reason, your children aren't home. The void of sound is so refreshing that you lose yourself in it.

But as time passes by, what you thought was true peace becomes longing; a longing for your children to disturb your calm... not because it gratifies you, but because you love them and their presence in your life.

And somehow, all the commotion they build also brings you peace. This peace is in knowing where they are and what they are doing... that they are safe.

The Fruitful Mom knows peace doesn't always look like a day at the spa, it can also look like a mother singing while dishes clatter, loud laughter, and when thoughts jumble on top of the other from all the background noise children make playing.

For true peace is not found in the silence of an ideal moment, but it is in the revelation that Jesus is the Prince of Peace; that His peace will sustain you in any tribulation.

God's Peace: A Guard for the Heart

Philippians 4:7 reveals that *"the peace of God, which transcends all understanding, will guard your hearts and your minds in Christ Jesus." (NIV)*

Having peace doesn't remove or take from your responsibilities as a mother; it safeguards you while you carry them. Peace makes it possible even when your thoughts start to unravel uncontrollably.

Just remember that peace is a choice of focus. It's shifting your eyes from the problem to the Promise; from the storm to the Savior.

The waves may not stop immediately, but when your gaze is fixed on Jesus, the struggles inside you begin to settle, even if it reaches your heart before your surroundings.

In the Shift

Some mothers have the tendency to become overwhelmed with meeting their own standards; they lose sight of what they have already accomplished, focusing on worrying about their shortcomings and what they weren't able to complete. This loss of focus steals peace.

As many have experienced, motherhood invites a thousand reasons to become restless in thoughts, like with the safety of her children, provisions, health concerns, the unknown future. Yet God never called mothers to be distressed. He called mothers to cast it upon Him in surrender, so that you can live in His daily peace.

Growing in God teaches the Fruitful Mom that peace is not the absence of conflict. It is the presence of Christ.

Walking in Peace

His peace is not something she waits for, it is something she walks in.

The Shoes of Peace steady her steps, guide her pace, and help her carry calm into every room she enters. When chaos rises around her, these shoes root her in the Gospel, so that she can spread God's Word.

Peace becomes her movement, not her escape.

The Shoes of Peace helps a mother take gentler steps with her children, walk patiently through difficult days, and stand firm even when life pushes hard.

It enables peace to also become her posture, and it turns rushed mornings into opportunities for grace.

The Shoes of Peace reminds the Fruitful Mom that she is not walking to peace, she is walking from within it, while carrying the Gospel everywhere she steps.

The more a mother walks in peace, the more she leaves footprints of calm direction for her children to follow.

Practicing Peace

Peace simply does not happen, it's practiced.

Sometimes peace looks like a deep breath when you close your eyes for three seconds before you answer. Sometimes it's choosing silence over an argument or laughter over irritation. Sometimes peace is an internal prayer given to the Lord instead of trying to fix what's not yours to fix.

These small choices become sacred habits that welcome peace into the everyday rhythm of motherhood.

The Fruitful Mom comes to know that peace is not found in the circumstantial, but in confidence, knowing Who holds it all together when she cannot.

When a mother makes room for the God of peace to step in, she realizes that peace isn't the result of your environment; it's the result of trusting the One who produces it.

Your children learn to trust not because life is hard or easy, but because they see you anchored in Someone greater than life itself.

When Peace Is Shaken

There will also be moments when your children pull peace right out from under you; with their words, choices, or disruptions, causing unexpected frustration that builds up...

Then in an instant... boom! The explosion of uncontrolled emotions release.

All it took was that one more thing like a tantrum, an argument, a spill, or a slammed door from an angry child who is refusing to listen.

In those moments, remember this: peace is not gone, it's just misplaced. Feelings are fleeting, but when emotions flare, the Spirit of God remains unchanging.

The Fruitful Mom adheres to not get lost in the temporary rise of frustration, but to breathe and remember Who walks beside her.

As a mother, understand that there will also be days when you believe you've lost your peace completely, causing tears to blur into your prayers and thoughts. But this too shall pass, as you make the effort to remember who you are in Christ. Only in Him, can you stand firm in the sovereignty of God, because peace is not a condition. It is a Person.

The world's peace depends on circumstances; God's peace depends on your connection with Him.

Jesus said, *"Peace I leave with you; my peace I give you. I do not give to you as the world gives. Do not let your hearts be troubled and do not be afraid."*

John 14:27 (NIV)

Stay connected and His peace is yours.

Peace That Protects

Peace is also a weapon; one of the most underestimated in a mother's spiritual armor.

Ephesians 6:15 tells us to have our *"feet fitted with the readiness that comes from the gospel of peace."*

These are not slippers of comfort; they are boots of warfare.

When these boots are on, it allows a mother to stand her ground when trials try to overtake her home. When she chooses peace, she refuses to let fear or frustration dictate her steps.

Peace gives her traction on slippery ground. It keeps her steady when the enemy tries to make her stumble.

Every act of humility, every word spoken in calm instead of shouted, every decision to trust instead of panic is a spiritual stance of victory. Peace is not passive. It's active, an overcoming force that silences the enemy and restores order to your family.

Unfortunately, the world only sees peace as calm, but it's actually a force guided by faith and power. In God's hands, peace is fierce; it protects, it strengthens, it sustains.

These boots are not made of weakness but wisdom. They are not for retreat but readiness. They are used to march into action and defend what God has promised is yours.

Ripples of Peace

The same peace you cultivate within your spirit becomes the peace your children carry into their own worlds. They'll remember the sound of your steady voice when life feels loud. They'll recall the way you chose patience over anger and critical judgment.

Peace, like love, has a ripple effect that outlasts the moment.

So, take notice, the enemy cannot thrive where peace remains. That's why he tries so hard to disturb it.

He doesn't need to destroy your home; he only needs to distract your mind. But the Fruitful Mom stands firm, knowing that every time she chooses peace, she denies the enemy access to her spirit and home.

Peace armors her journey and readies her stance. It keeps her moving forward when everything around tries to pull her back into a pool of doubt and frustrations.

Know, that the same God who calmed the sea, is still the same God today. Give Him every anxious thought that attempts to steal your peace. Let your confidence in God become an altar you lay at His feet.

Peace That Stays

Having peace does not mean everything is entirely in order. It means you are no longer controlled by the disruptive atmosphere around you.

It means you've learned to find stillness in hardship, confidence in surrender, and strength in the One who never wavers.

"You will keep in perfect peace those whose minds are steadfast, because they trust in you." Isaiah 26:3 (NIV)

Peace isn't about what surrounds you; it's about what sustains you.

When you trust God with every piece of your heart, He guards your life with every ounce of His peace.

And from that calm assurance, something beautiful begins to grow with forbearance.

Forbearance is peace stretched through time; the proof that what you've planted in stillness will bloom in God's perfect season. It is the slow unfolding of trust, the willingness to wait while God works on your behalf. As peace steadies the heart, fortitude strengthens the spirit.

Because where peace teaches you to be still, fortitude teaches you to stay.

It's the quiet endurance that says, "I will not rush what God is still writing." And from that waiting, the next fruit begins to take shape... **patience.**

Closing Reflection

Let peace settle over you like a quiet covering, God guards what you place in His hands.

Personal Insight

Peace used to feel like something I needed to chase, something fragile that could slip away at any moment. Over time, I've learned that peace is less about what is happening around me and more about Who I am resting in.

There have been moments when fear pressed in hard and anxiety tried to take control, yet God whispered calm into my heart when I chose to trust Him. Peace has become my reminder that I don't have to carry everything; I just have to place everything in God's hands. And in that surrender, my soul breathes again.

Moments of Reflection

1. What would change in your home if peace became your first response instead of your last resort?

2. How do your children see and learn peace through your reactions, tones, or routines?

3. Which worries are you still trying to carry on your own that God has asked you to cast onto Him?

4. What does "putting on the Shoes of Peace" look like in your everyday life?

5. How might surrender, not control, bring more calm to your heart and your household?

Prayer for Peace

Father,

Thank You for being the God who speaks "Peace, be still" over every storm in my life and in my home. When my mind feels crowded and my heart grows heavy, help me remember that peace is not found in perfection or control, but in surrendering to Your presence.

Teach me to breathe before reacting, to pray before panicking, and to rest in the truth that You are nearer than any anxious thought.

Guard my heart from fear, my mind from chaos, and my spirit from striving. Help me create a refuge of calm for my children, not by my own strength, but by Your Spirit working gently within me.

Let Your peace settle over my home like a blanket of grace and remind me daily that the One who holds the universe gently holds me too.

In Jesus' name,

Amen.

Chapter Four
PATIENCE is Trust in Slow Bloom

Wait for the Lord,
Be strong, and
Let your heart take courage;
Wait for the Lord!

Psalm 27:14

Patience in Waiting

In the biblical context, patience is long-suffering, endurance, and willingness to faithfully wait without angst or anger. It is learning not to be quick in your reactions and knowing how to control your tongue.

As many have experienced, controlling one's reaction to any given situation takes practice, especially if the other party is loose with theirs. You do not have control over others, but you do have control over the way you react and interact with them.

As mothers, patience can easily be lost at any given moment for any given reason. It may be the first or the last thing to go. Either way, mothers should practice with all their hearts to become steadfast with patience.

Mothers need to rehearse patience consistently.

This practice will unfold your trust and willingness to wait on the Lord as He works on your behalf.

When Progress Feels Invisible

A mother's world is built around waiting... waiting for little feet to grow, for hearts to understand, for prayers to be answered.

Yet, in the waiting, God is doing His most transformative work. He shapes a mother's spirit not through what happens quickly, but through what takes time.

His patience in you is proof that you are maturing in your walk with God, even if you are struggling with it, and even if you don't see it at first.

Where peace teaches you to rest in God, patience teaches you to hold fast to your words and actions. It's the holy art of believing in God.

Patience is a shielded faith; the quiet confidence that God is working even when a mother sees nothing changing.

The Shield of Faith protects her from the fiery darts of impatience, frustration, and discouragement. Every time she chooses not to snap, not to rush, not to push ahead of God, she lifts that shield.

Patience becomes an act of trust, a declaration that God's timing is wiser than her urgency. With the shield raised, she learns to breathe, wait, and believe that unseen seeds are still growing beneath the surface.

The Unseen Works of God

Patience isn't idle; it is the discipline of spiritual strength. It's holding your ground when nothing seems to move, believing that unseen roots are deepening even when there are no blossoms in sight.

The Fruitful Mom determines that patience is not about endurance for endurance's sake; it's about belief. Every delay, every "not yet," becomes a sacred space where confidence matures and dependence on God grows stronger.

When a mother prays and sees no immediate change in her child, her marriage, or her circumstances, patience whispers, "God is still working, hold fast in His Word."

It reminds her that His timing is perfect, no matter how long or short it may seem. She cannot control it. Just as a seed cannot rush its bloom, neither can she rush God's design.

The waiting is not wasted; it's preparing her for the harvest and teaching her to accept God's will, no matter the outcome.

Patience grows in the pauses... in the long nights, in unanswered prayers, and the moments when angst tempts mothers to falter in their responsibilities or gestures.

It grows when she persistently chooses to stay in God's Word, no matter the circumstances.

Patience doesn't erase pain or pressure; it refines how we walk through them. It's what turns tension into trust and delay into devotion.

Humbling Slow Seasons

There is something sacred about slow seasons... those in-between spaces where progress feels invisible and prayers echo longer than you hoped. They are not signs of God's absence but invitations to intimacy.

Patience is the classroom where faith learns to grow. It's where the mother's hands, so used to fixing, finally rest long enough for God's hands to move.

God invites mothers not to tighten their grip, but to loosen their concerns. Trust opens doors for Him to move.

Patience in a Fast-Paced World

In today's world, patience has become one of the hardest fruits to keep alive.

Life moves faster than ever, especially with schedules packed with school events, sports, and doctor's appointments; meals ordered and groceries delivered in minutes; answers found instantly with a swipe or a search. Convenience has replaced the slow process that once taught us to wait. And in that speed, something sacred has quietly thinned... our patience.

We now live in a society that rewards immediacy and measures worth by productivity. But the Spirit grows in the opposite direction, in God's timing, the unseen, the surrendered.

The Fruitful Mom must remember that fast doesn't always mean productivity. What blooms quickly often fades just as fast, but what grows slowly sends roots deep enough to endure any situation.

The Fruitful Mom comes to realize that impatience often springs from fear; fear that time is running out, that she's not doing enough, or that things won't turn out right. But patience dismantles fear by reminding her that God is never late.

He is the Keeper of time and the Author of growth. Every second surrendered to Him becomes holy ground where peace and faith intertwine.

When Patience Feels Impossible

There will be days when patience feels unattainable, when tempers flare, when progress feels invisible, when children test limits, or life feels unfair.

In those moments, patience isn't about pretending everything's fine by wiping away hidden tears shed in silence or solitude.

It's about not complaining.

Sometimes patience feels like watching a sunrise through fog; you know light is coming, but the haze blurs the horizon. You keep watching anyway because faith tells you it's there.

Motherhood is much the same. You wait through long days and hurried nights, trusting that the light of God's faithfulness will break through when it's time, praying that weariness never clouds your memory of His wisdom.

His patience also protects love from fading and joy from running dry. It bridges the gap between what is and what will be.

A Fruitful Mom shows her children how to endure, how to hope, and how to trust a God whose plans are good, even when unknown. It's the understanding that she is sustained in God's strength. It is the knowing that one day she will bear the fruit of everything she believed in.

Trusting God's Timing

James 5:7 reminds us, *"Be patient, then, brothers and sisters, until the Lord's coming. See how the farmer waits for the land to yield its valuable crop, patiently waiting for the autumn and spring rains."*

Like the farmer, the Fruitful Mom must trust that what has been promised will happen, not on her schedule, but on God's.

Her task is not to force the bloom, but to tend the soil with consistency and faith. The soil is her children, the tender hearts God lovingly placed within her care, to water with prayer, nurture with patience, and trust Him to bring forth in His time.

And just as farmers trust the rhythm of seasons, mothers must trust the rhythm of God's timing in their homes. Every season has a purpose: the early rain softens the ground, and the latter rain brings the harvest.

Patience teaches her to value both.

Patience as Worship

Patience is the slow dance between promise and fulfillment. It's the quiet confidence that every delay carries divine design. While the world rushes toward instant results, the Fruitful Mom walks at heaven's pace, knowing that growth in her children and in herself takes time. The same hands that hold her children hold the seasons of her life, restoring and accelerating time itself on behalf of her faithfulness.

And when she feels weary in the waiting, when progress seems invisible, God whispers: *"Do not grow weary in doing good, for at the proper time you will reap a harvest if you do not give up."* Galatians 6:9 (NIV)

Patience doesn't just wait; it waits well.

It waits with worship, with gratitude, with faith anchored in a faithful God. It is less about enduring time and more about embracing transformation.

Patience gathers all the fruits before it, love, joy, and peace, and stretches them into lasting resilience. Love gives patience its motive, joy gives it strength, and peace gives it calm.

Together they create a mother who endures with grace because God is good.

Patience That Shapes Legacy

In the heart of a patient mother lives the quiet confidence that God is writing something beautiful, not only in her children's lives but in her own.

Each delay refines her, each pause reshapes her, each unanswered prayer deepens her trust. Patience doesn't just grow something around her; it grows something within her... a strength that doesn't shake when life does.

In motherhood, patience is the gentle strength that turns ordinary days into sacred opportunities.

It teaches her to reflect before correcting, to pray before reacting, and to trust before understanding.

And as patience matures, it gives birth to something lasting and strong... **kindness**.

For kindness is what patience looks like when it touches others.

Closing Reflection

Patience blooms slowly and needs to be intentionally practiced. Trust that God is growing something beautiful in you, even if you can't see it yet.

Personal Insight

Patience has been one of the hardest fruits for me to grow. There were days I wished change would come faster—in my children, in my circumstances, and even in myself. But God has used waiting seasons to shape me deeply.

He reminded me that waiting is not wasted when it is placed in His hands. Some of the most beautiful things in motherhood take time, and some prayers bloom slowly.

Patience has become God's invitation for me to trust Him more than my timelines, to breathe instead of rush, and to believe that His timing is not only right. It is loving. It has taught me that God's timing is perfect.

Moments of Reflection

1. Where in your life is God asking you to wait in His patience instead of worry?

2. What small daily choices could help you "wait well" instead of growing weary?

3. How does patience shape the way you respond to your children, especially on hard days?

4. What would it look like to see waiting not as delay, but as divine preparation?

5. How might God be strengthening your patience through what feels slow, silent, or unfinished in this season?

Prayer for Patience

Lord,

Thank You for walking with me through every moment that stretches me and every season that slows me.

When my plans feel delayed, my strength feels thin, and my patience feels tested, teach me to lean not on my own ability, but on Your unfailing grace. Help me breathe before reacting, listen before correcting, and trust before worrying.

Teach me to be slow to speak and open to understanding.

Remind me that patience is not passive; it is worship in motion, faith made visible, and love choosing to wait. Shape my heart to wait with hope, to respond with gentleness, and to rest in knowing that You are always working, even when I cannot see it. Strengthen me as I mother, so that my children see patience not as an act of weakness, but as perseverance rooted in You.

Lord, grow in me a spirit that is slow to anger and rich in compassion, and let Your peace steady me in the moments when I feel rushed, overwhelmed, or undone. I surrender my timing for Yours.

Teach me to wait well, to endure with grace, and to trust that every delay in Your hands is full of purpose.

In Jesus' name,

Amen.

Chapter Five
KINDNESS is Love in Motion

Be kind to one another,
Tenderhearted,
Forgiving one another, as
God in Christ forgave you.

Ephesians 4:32

What Kindness Really Is

Kindness is what love looks like when it's lived out loud. It's compassion clothed in action; the gentle strength that chooses tenderness over tension, grace over grievance.

For the Fruitful Mom, kindness is not a reaction; it's a reflection of the One who is endlessly kind toward her.

Kindness That Changes Atmospheres

Kindness begins where impatience ends. It's the respectful answer that diffuses anger, the listening ear that restores peace, and the gentle tone that reminds your child they are safe even after correction.

True kindness doesn't depend on how others act; it flows from who God is within you. It's the quiet power that turns ordinary days into sanctified encounters.

Ephesians 4:32 says, *"Be kind and compassionate to one another, forgiving each other, just as in Christ God forgave you."*

This verse becomes a mother's quiet anthem. She implements it with her children and remembers to apply it to herself when her children choose to do what they shouldn't.

Kindness Doesn't Mean Weakness

It's the courage to stay tender in a harsh world, to hold truth in one hand and mercy in the other. It's speaking correction without crushing, choosing empathy over irritation, and remembering that every person, even her child, is a work in progress, just as she is.

Kindness is not softness without structure. It is strength wrapped in truth.

The Belt of Truth keeps a mother grounded, centered, and aligned when emotions try to sway her. Kindness guided by truth has boundaries, clarity, and purpose.

It allows her to speak gently without enabling, to correct lovingly without crushing, and to be firm without being harsh. When she fastens this belt each day, she is anchoring her heart in honesty, her tone in grace, and her interactions in God's wisdom.

Truth strengthens kindness so it becomes both tender and trustworthy.

Kindness in Action

Sometimes kindness is being soft-spoken instead of direct. Other times it's understanding when to remain silent as others are belligerent, and choosing not to respond in retaliation when others instigate contention.

It's a meal prepared with love when the family forgets to say thank you. It's praying for a child who's closed off rather than trying to control them.

True kindness is not reactive; it's reflective. It reflects the heart of Christ: patient, merciful, and unshakably good.

As the Fruitful Mom continues to grow, she becomes more aware that she abides in His presence.

This helps kindness flow more naturally out of her. It's not something she creates; it's something that overflows through the Spirit of God within her.

This isn't only for when life is calm; it's a call for when life feels turbulent. Kindness has the strength to quiet difficult seasons when words fall short.

But in the moments where kindness is hard to find due to emotions running high, remember you are created in God's image, and you have dominion of what words and expressions come out of your mouth.

It is in these times that the actions you choose to display hold the most power. They reveal what's inside your heart.

Kindness also restores what harshness breaks. One kind word can undo hours of tension; one act of grace can mend what impatience frayed. Kindness has a way of rebuilding bridges that frustration burns down.

"For the mouth speaks what the heart is full of" Matthew 12:34 (NIV)

In motherhood, kindness often looks like doing unnoticed things, wiping the counter again, forgiving the same offense, or showing up when you'd rather rest. It's unseen work to the people around you, but heaven sees it all. God treasures every act of love done in His name, even the smallest ones.

When a mother chooses kindness over resentment because of her child's disobedience, her spirit becomes a conduit for God's healing, not only for herself, but for those around her.

In those moments, kindness becomes a choice of strength, not softness. It takes courage to stay gentle when you feel pulled apart, to hold your tongue when you want to shout, and to serve when you'd rather withdraw.

Yet, it is in those very moments that the Fruitful Mom most resembles Christ.

Colossians 3:12 reminds us, *"Clothe yourselves with compassion, kindness, humility, gentleness, and patience."*

To dress yourself in kindness is to make it your covering, not a mood or moment, but a mindset. It becomes how you walk, how you speak, and how you respond.

Kindness in a Harsh World

In today's world, kindness has become a rarity. It has been replaced by quick tempers, harsh comments, and hurried hearts.

Technology has sped up communication but slowed down compassion. The internet has made it easier for people to say what they would never say face to face, hiding behind screens that separate hearts.

Words are flung without thought, and opinions are posted without grace. The disconnect between people, especially as phones and screens begin to raise children more than conversations do, has hardened hearts and dulled empathy.

In a culture where self-gratification often outweighs self-control, kindness feels almost foreign.

Sensitivity toward others has nearly vanished, but the Fruitful Mom carries a countercultural calling: to bring softness into sharp spaces.

Her kind response becomes a ripple that pushes back the current of cruelty and engulfs her children in a light that softens what the world hardens, reminding them that kindness still has the power to heal what cruelty breaks.

Modeling Kindness at Home

Kindness teaches children what mercy feels like.

It shows them that being strong doesn't mean being loud, and that being right doesn't mean being inconsiderate. They learn through their mother's example that kindness isn't about getting credit; it's about carrying character and caring for others even if it is undeserved.

The Fruitful Mom knows that kindness starts at home but is meant to overflow beyond it, to the teacher, the neighbor, and the stranger in the store. Her children will notice when she pauses to listen, helps without recognition, or offers a word of blessing instead of complaint.

These moments are seeds planted into their hearts, teaching them that kindness isn't something we do for attention, but for eternity.

When she becomes elderly, a mother hopes her children will show her the same love and care she blessed them with as they were being raised. And if she wasn't all that she could have been, she can hope in God and ask forgiveness for her mishaps.

God will restore and soften once bitter hearts and reunite families once again. With kindness, that is more than possible.

Being Kind to Yourself

Sometimes mothers can become very judgmental with who they are and what they have become; quietly criticizing their actions for not being enough, doing enough, or meeting their own expectations.

The same voice that soothes her child in moments of fear or misunderstandings must also learn to soothe her own heart. The same compassion a mother so freely gives to others must be turned inward; reminding her that grace unreceived cannot flow freely.

To walk in this kindness, a mother must let God's gentleness reach the places within her that still believe they have to earn His love. She must learn to fall back on patience to remain in His kindness.

Kindness: The Thread that Binds the Fruits Together

Kindness is the invisible glue that holds love, patience, and peace together.

It's like water to the soil of the soul, quiet, steady, unseen, yet essential for every other fruit to grow. It's what turns faith into fruit. It's not loud or proud, but its impact is lasting.

The tone of kindness can linger long after the words are gone. It becomes the tune her children hum in their own homes someday.

Small Kindnesses That Make a Big Difference

Kindness doesn't need to be mutual; it just needs one person to participate. Because one act of grace can shift the entire atmosphere of any place, especially a home.

Kindness spreads like a fire, warming the hearts of those around us with every act, every smile, every prayer, and every pause that becomes a sermon of grace spoken without words.

When a mother kneels to her child's level to correct with love instead of judgment, she mirrors the Father's heart: firm, but full of mercy. Her voice becomes the echo of grace that teaches, heals, and guides.

When she chooses kindness again and again, it becomes her language of love, her rhythm of faith, and her ministry to the world. Because kindness, once rooted, doesn't stop branching out.

It spreads and becomes goodness in action. It grows like tender vines around the hearts of others, drawing them in and inspiring them to extend the kindness they've received.

God's compassion is not weakness; it's wisdom.

It sees beyond behavior and reaches for the heart.

His kindness is also what keeps love alive in hard seasons.

It's the hand that still reaches across the distance after an argument, the note slipped into a lunchbox that says, "I believe in you," the grace that says, "Lets start over." It's the small, sacred gestures that whisper, "I see you, and I choose to love you anyway."

Kindness in Discipline

Even in discipline, kindness leads. It doesn't ignore truth; it delivers it with gentleness. It doesn't excuse wrong; it offers restoration.

Proverbs 31:26 says, *"She speaks with wisdom, and faithful instruction is on her tongue."* A mother's kindness is the language her children will remember as they age.

Kindness is love, refined through patience and expressed through peace.

It's what gives love a face and peace a sound. It softens the hard edges of family life, turning correction into connection and commotion into compassion. It transforms duty into delight because it shifts the focus from what you do to how you do it.

The Fruitful Mom also knows that her kindness carries generational weight.

The words she speaks over her children, words of blessing, belief, and grace, shape how they see themselves and others. A single, kind word can reroute a discouraged heart, restore a broken moment, or rewrite a family memory.

Kindness That Leaves a Legacy

Kindness lingers long after the moment passes.

It echoes in the heart like a cadence of mercy, replayed in the lives of those who received it, and in those echoes, something begins to grow in patience, gentleness, and strength. It's a mother's **goodness**.

Because kindness, when fully lived, becomes goodness in action, the next fruit of a life rooted deeply in God.

Closing Reflection

Kindness doesn't need ideal circumstances to count. One gentle word today can change the tone of your home tomorrow.

Personal Insight

There were times I believed kindness meant always being gentle with others, yet I struggled to extend it to myself. Motherhood can be demanding, and it is easy to become harsh with yourself. God had to teach me that kindness begins inside my own thoughts.

As I learned to receive His grace, I became more able to offer grace to others. Kindness is the evidence of compassion. It is choosing softness when the world expects hardness. It is God's way of reminding us how to treat others as we wish to be treated ourselves.

Moments of Reflection

1. When was the last time someone's kindness changed the direction of your day? How might you offer that same gift to someone else this week?

2. Are there moments when kindness feels more like sacrifice than ease? What would it look like to see those moments as opportunities for strength instead of strain?

3. How can you model kindness in your home when frustration or exhaustion tries to take over your words or actions?

4. Have you been kinder to others than to yourself lately? What would it look like to extend God's grace to your own heart today?

5. Where might God be inviting you to show kindness that heals in your family, friendships, or even toward someone difficult to love?

Prayer for Kindness

Lord,

Make my heart tender and my words gentle. Teach me to see others through Your eyes, especially in the moments when frustration rises and patience runs thin.

Help me choose kindness when it feels inconvenient, unnoticed, or unreturned. Let compassion lead my tone, grace steady my reactions, and mercy soften my judgments. Fill my home with a spirit of kindness that restores, rebuilds, and reassures.

May my children learn through my example that strength is not loud but loving; not forceful, but faithful. Where irritation tries to settle, plant kindness.

Where impatience tries to grow, plant understanding. Where pride wants to speak first, teach me humility. Lord, let kindness be my instinct, my language, and my legacy. Let it reflect Your heart through every word and every act of love.

Make my hands gentle, my heart warm, and my presence a reminder of Your goodness. Let others see You in me.

In Jesus' name,

Amen.

Chapter Six
GOODNESS is Doing What's Right When No One is Looking

When Goodness Costs You

Goodness is the quiet courage that chooses what honors God over what pleases the moment. It is kindness strengthened by conviction, compassion shaped by purpose, and love lived faithfully in the solitude of your mind.

For the Fruitful Mom, goodness is not about performance.

It is about how her attitude aligns with the heart of God.

Goodness is the daily turning of a mother's heart toward what is right, even when she feels weary. It shows up in truths spoken in mercy and is demonstrated in forgiveness before resentment settles.

This goodness rarely announces itself, yet it becomes the invisible scaffolding of her home.

Her children may not understand its depth now, but the steadiness they feel is shaped by the quiet righteousness she practices when the world is not looking.

Goodness grows in the unseen, yet it bears fruit in every season.

Goodness in the Hidden Places

Goodness means living with wholeness; being the same in the stillness of your home as you are in the presence of others.

In a world that elevates image over integrity, goodness becomes sacred resistance. It's the choice to be rooted in God instead of performing for others. It is authentic instead of calculating personal benefits.

Children absorb truth before they ever understand it. They watch how their mother responds to stress, how she speaks behind closed doors, and how she prays when her mental capacity feels stretched. They see whether her Sunday devotion reflects her Monday decisions.

A mother's consistency becomes a quiet sermon; one they read with their eyes long before they can read Scripture with their words.

This kind of goodness gives them deep assurance.

They feel safe because her character does not shift with mood, audience, or circumstance.

Through her steadiness, they begin to understand the heart of God Himself, faithful, unchanging, and good in every season.

Goodness in Motion

Goodness is righteousness in motion; the visible expression of a heart aligned with God.

Paired with the Breastplate of Righteousness, goodness protects a mother's integrity from compromise.

It guards her in hidden moments of temptation, discouragement, or inconsistency. When she wears this armor, she chooses to be the same in private as she is in public.

Her goodness becomes a covering over her character; an anchored moral compass her family can rely on.

With the breastplate in place, her actions reflect purity, honesty, and the steady goodness of God.

Unwavering Goodness

Galatians 6:9 reminds us, *"Let us not become weary in doing good..."*

Goodness is not a moment; it is a rhythm.

It appears in the small tasks no one sees:

- the meals prepared with love,

- the whispered prayers over a sleeping child,

- the firm-yet-tender correction that shapes more than behavior, and

- the quiet decisions that place obedience above ease.

These simple acts become seeds heaven never overlooks. Ordinary to the world but endearing to God.

Courage Wrapped in Grace

Goodness has a tender face, but it also has a straight spine.

It takes holy courage to remain anchored when culture drifts, to choose purity over popularity, reverence over compromise, conviction over convenience.

Goodness is not swayed by pressure. It is guided by purpose.

Sometimes goodness whispers gently.

Sometimes it stands firm.

But it always honors God.

When the World Presses In

There will be moments when goodness costs you something.

When you walk away from gossip instead of adding to it...

When you apologize first, even when pride resists...

When you set a boundary, others misunderstand...

Sometimes choosing good means releasing friendships, habits, or environments that no longer honor who God is shaping you to be. And that release can feel like loss. But goodness aligned with Scripture is never wasted.

Never miscounted.

Never forgotten.

What feels heavy today may be the very thing protecting your legacy tomorrow.

What feels costly may become the spiritual inheritance of your children. Goodness may stretch you, but it will not fail you.

Goodness That Guides

When your child asks, "Why can't we do that?" and your answer is simply, "Because it is inappropriate and it does not honor God," a holy moment unfolds.

You're not teaching rules.

You're teaching reverence for the One who created all things.

Goodness becomes the light that guides their steps, teaching them to discern not only between right and wrong, but between what is good and what is almost good.

Your conviction becomes their compass.

Your surrender becomes their safety.

Goodness becomes the language of your home.

The Fruitful Mom learns that moments like these are more than conversations... they are quiet discipleship.

She realizes she is not simply correcting behavior but shaping her child's world-view. Each time she answers with conviction and gentleness, she is teaching her child that goodness flows from devotion, not duty.

Rooted in God's Goodness

Psalm 23:6 declares, *"Surely goodness and mercy shall follow me…"*

A mother rooted in God's goodness doesn't force goodness. She reflects on it.

It flows through her tone, her decisions, her patience, and her presence.

Her home feels like a sanctuary, a place where truth and grace coexist, where peace lingers, and where her children sense, without explanation, that God lives there.

Goodness becomes the quiet fragrance of a Spirit-led life.

A Legacy That Lasts

Goodness is not an image to maintain. It is a legacy to leave.

Your children will remember:

- the sound of grace in their home,

- the way forgiveness felt safe,

- the steady calm that wrapped around them like warmth.

These memories become the foundation of their own walk with God.

Every small act of goodness becomes a steppingstone they carry into adulthood.

And as the Fruitful Mom walks in goodness day after day, something deeper takes root: **faithfulness**; the next fruit growing naturally from consistency, integrity, and surrendered obedience.

Closing Reflection

Goodness grows in private places. Choose what honors God in secret and trust Him to bring the fruit in due time.

Personal Insight

Goodness has challenged me to live consistently; not only in public moments, but in private ones, when only God and my family see. There have been times I wondered if the unseen efforts even mattered.

But God has shown me that goodness planted in secret grows deeply. Goodness has reminded me that I don't live to please people; I live to honor God. And that changes everything.

Moments of Reflection

1. Where do you find it hardest to do good when you know no one is watching?

2. How can you demonstrate goodness to your children this week through action, not just words?

3. What does it mean to you that "goodness and mercy will follow you"?

4. Is there an area of your life where doing good feels unnoticed or unappreciated? How might you see it as worship to God instead of work?

5. Has goodness ever cost you something like comfort, approval, relationships, or convenience? How did God meet you in that place, or how can you trust Him to meet you now?

Prayer for Goodness

Father,

Shape my heart to desire what is good, pure, and pleasing to You. Let goodness not be something I only *do*, but who I become through Your Spirit living in me.

Teach me to love righteousness, to delight in truth, and to walk in integrity even when no one is watching. Help me choose what honors You over what comforts me.

Let my actions reflect Your character: patient, just, merciful, and tender in spirit.

May goodness flow through my decisions, my discipline, my conversations, and my quiet thoughts. When temptation to compromise arises, strengthen my resolve. When negativity tries to darken my spirit, fill me with Your light.

Let my children learn goodness not by hearing rules, but by witnessing a life surrendered to You. Lord, make my home a place where goodness feels safe, familiar, and expected because Your presence is here.

In Jesus' name,

Amen.

Chapter Seven
FAITHFULNESS is Standing Firm When You Feel Faint

Faithfulness in the Quiet Places

A mother's faithfulness is one of the most overlooked virtues. It doesn't shine or demand acknowledgment. To truly see it, one must pay attention to the small behaviors and subtle consistencies where her devotion lives.

Faithfulness begins in the deep places of a mother's heart and thoughts and is quietly expressed through her actions as she completes her day.

For the Fruitful Mom, faithfulness isn't measured by how boldly she serves, but by how her character reveals her commitment.

Faithful in the Small Things

Motherhood is where faithfulness hides inside the ordinary.

It appears in the morning routines, the late-night prayers, the tears that were quietly wiped away, in meals prepared with love, and in the decisions made with eternity in mind.

Most of her faithful moments will never be acknowledged on Earth. But heaven counts each one.

What she does in secret is never forgotten by the God who sees. Her daily sacrifices become seeds of spiritual inheritance, quiet acts of devotion that shape her children far more deeply than she realizes.

When You Feel Overlooked

Some callings come with titles, awards, or applause.

Motherhood is not usually one of them.

A mother pours herself out day after day, yet the fruit of her labor grows slowly... almost completely hidden like roots beneath the soil.

And since a mother's efforts are not always acknowledged, she begins to wonder, "Are my prayers working? Is what I can do even enough? Do I make any difference at all?"

But God sees what she cannot.

He sees her choosing patience instead of anger. He sees her holding a tired child instead of holding onto frustration. He sees her praying for their future even when fear speaks louder.

Her reward is not recognition, but God's affirmation.

Faithfulness and the Shield of Faith

Faithfulness is perseverance wrapped in belief.

It is waking up each day and choosing to keep going, not because motherhood is easy, but because God is steady.

Paired with the Shield of Faith, faithfulness helps her block the whispers: "You're not enough. Nothing is changing. Your efforts don't matter."

This shield doesn't just defend her... it strengthens her resolve.

Faithfulness becomes her testimony.

She stays. She prays. She shows up. She trusts, not by her strength, but by faith that God is working in every moment.

Strength That Stays

Faithfulness is not glamorous. It is grit wrapped in grace.

It rises not from willpower but from the Holy Spirit within her.

Drawing from Scripture, believers are called to wear faithfulness as part of their character not as performers, but as an extension of the character of God who stands firm; never shifting or changing.

A mother's faithfulness flows from His. Her strength grows from His nearness.

The more she leans on God, the more faithfulness becomes a natural rhythm rather than an exhausting effort.

Faithfulness Tested

Motherhood will test her... often.

Fatigue, interruptions, emotional heaviness, loneliness, and unexpected storms press against her resolve.

Yet these same pressures deepen her dependence on God... in every prayer lifted when she wants to give up, in every moment she remains patient when her feelings urge retreat, and in every choice to love when her heart feels bruised.

These become sacred offerings to God.

Her consistency forms a rhythm heaven recognizes, a devotion building something eternal.

The God Who Remains

Faithfulness begins in the heart that whispers:

"I will keep showing up, even when I am tired."

It measures success not by speed, but by steadfastness.

Her life becomes a quiet reflection of God's constancy; in the way she comforts, in the way she guides, in the way she forgives, and in the way she stays.

Her faithfulness becomes a living reminder to her children that God is enduring, steady, and always present.

The Faithfulness That Shapes Your Children

Faithfulness reframes the mundane into the sacred. It reminds her that washing dishes, driving carpools, preparing meals, and speaking truth in love are not interruptions to her calling... they are her calling.

Motherhood is not a "lesser occupation."

It is a God-given ministry that shapes generations.

Her faithfulness plants seed her children will harvest long after she is gone.

Through her steadiness, they learn: love stays, commitments matter, and God can be trusted because trust was modeled in her.

Faithfulness That Bears Fruit Over Time

My husband once asked me, "What if your calling is to raise your children?"

To my surprise, the question unsettled me. I didn't want my calling to be *only* motherhood, even though I knew how valuable it is. My reaction revealed something deeper: I had forgotten how God defines success.

Somewhere along the way, I began measuring my value by what I could produce instead of who I was in Christ. I didn't realize my perspective had been shaped more by the world's standards than by God's truth.

Culture tells women fulfillment exists outside the home. That progress means production. That motherhood should be supplemented, not centered.

But God shifted my heart.

I realized my children, their futures, their faith, and their souls are worth far more than anything I could achieve for myself.

And even though not every mother can stay home, every mother has been entrusted with shaping the eternal souls of the children they had helped to create.

Heaven measures that differently than the world does.

Difficult Realizations

When motherhood feels overwhelmingly difficult, I often stop and ask myself:

"What is the alternative? Would stepping away undo what I've built? How would it affect my children now... and in their future as Christians?"

Those questions bring clarity.

Even on the hardest days, my children and their well-being are reason enough to remind me to stay faithful.

Mothers need to remember that relying on personal resilience leads only so far.

It is the reliance on God that leads a mother farther than she imagined possible.

A personal relationship with God becomes essential here; it is the anchor that steadies her beliefs. The deeper she knows Him, the easier it becomes to remain faithful, because she has experienced the unshakable faithfulness of God Himself.

Letting Go of Control

A mother's desire to protect can quietly transform into a desire to control. But faithfulness invites her to release what she cannot shape.

When she tries to hold everything together by herself, her home grows weary under the weight. But when she entrusts her children to the God who formed them, peace takes root.

Boundaries covered in love, guidance grounded in prayer, and room to grow. These become the tools God uses to shape her children.

A Life That Can Be Trusted

Faithfulness means becoming someone her children can rely on; consistent in character, steady in love, honest about weakness, quick to apologize, and safe to confide in.

Her unseen decisions shape their understanding of trust.

Her follow-through shapes their understanding of responsibility.

Her humility shapes their understanding of grace.

Faithfulness is not merely a trait. It is a testimony.

Love That Perseveres

Faithfulness is not built in grand moments. It grows in subtle increments of intentional choices by choosing forgiveness over bitterness, hope over discouragement, prayer over despair, and presence over withdrawal.

Faithfulness does not ask for perfection, only that she rises again. A mother's strength is not her own. God takes her commitment and turns it into resilience.

When the Path Feels Foggy

Some days faithfulness feels like walking through fog, seeing nothing ahead, yet taking another step toward God.

This is surrender.

This is trust.

This is faithfulness in action.

Even when she is faithless, *God "remains faithful"*. 2 Timothy 2:13 (NIV)

And in that steadfast dependence, faithfulness becomes a rich soil where something new begins to grow... **gentleness**.

Closing Reflection

Every faithful step you take, tired, quiet, and in private, is heard in heaven and woven into eternity.

Personal Insight

There were seasons when I felt unseen and wondered whether my efforts mattered. It was in those quiet moments that God reminded me He sees every act of faithfulness.

Faithfulness is not built in grand gestures but in steady devotion: showing up, loving well, praying continually, and trusting God when outcomes aren't visible or what you expected.

Motherhood has taught me that faithfulness isn't about never feeling weary; it's about choosing to remain, even when I am. And in those moments, God strengthens me with His own faithfulness that carries me through my days.

Moments of Reflection

1. In what ways is God calling you to stay faithful when you feel weary?

2. What promises are you still holding onto that require trust in His timing?

3. How can you model faithfulness for your children in your words, actions, and commitments?

4. When have you seen God's faithfulness sustain you through a difficult season?

5. Is there an area of your life or motherhood where you've been trying to carry everything alone? What would it look like to entrust that place to God in faithfulness rather than in fear or frustration?

Prayer for Faithfulness

Lord,

Make me faithful in the small things, the unseen things, and in the everyday moments that build a legacy.

Strengthen my heart to stay committed when my feelings waver and when the path feels long. Help me to remain steady in love, consistent in prayer, and anchored in truth.

Teach me to show up with faith even when results are not immediate, and to trust Your timing above my own.

Let my yes mean yes, my promises hold weight, and my children see a mother who finishes what she begins, not by her own strength, but by Your Spirit.

When discouragement tries to whisper that my efforts are unnoticed, remind me that You see every seed I plant and every sacrifice I make. Turn my perseverance into worship, my routines into devotion, and my duty into delight.

May I reflect Your faithfulness (in my marriage), in my motherhood, and in every space, You place me.

In Jesus' name,

Amen.

Chapter Eight
GENTLENESS is Strength Under Control

*Therefore, as
God's chosen people, holy and dearly loved,
Clothe yourselves with compassion, kindness,
Humility, gentleness and patience*

Colossians 3:12

The Strength in Softness

Gentleness is not weakness. It is might harnessed by humility.

It's knowing you could be harsh but choosing to be kind. It's the calm in correction, the softness in the struggle, and the grace that steadies the home when everything feels fragile.

Gentleness is not the absence of authority. It's authority wrapped in warmth. It's the confidence that doesn't need to shout to be heard, because it speaks from peace, not pride.

This peace moves together with gentleness, shaping a mother's footsteps with calmness and compassion. When paired with the Shoes of Peace, gentleness guides her into conversations with calm, helps her correct her children without crushing their hearts, and allows her to move through difficult moments with grace instead of tension.

This teaches her to approach her home with steady, soft steps filled with Spirit-controlled strength.

Every gentle step taken becomes a peace-bearing step to wholeness.

Grace in Correction

The Fruitful Mom learns that gentleness is power submitted to peace. It's not about avoiding truth; it's about delivering truth in love.

Sometimes mothers can deliver truth too directly at their children, causing unintentional hurt or resentment. Gentleness allows correction to heal rather than inflicting emotional pain, to instruct without putting down, and to guide without humiliating.

It's the hand that wipes away tears without shaming; the patience that listens before lecturing, and the awareness that her tone often teaches more than her words.

When correction flows from calm instead of annoyance, it leaves room for both teaching and trust. It allows the child to be more open and understanding of the why's of the correction.

Children rarely remember every rule, but they always remember how they felt in their mother's presence. Gentleness ensures that what they remember most is love.

It's this gentleness that gives the Holy Spirit space to work in the child's heart, doing what anger never could.

It teaches that discipline isn't about dominance, but direction; helping them understand not just what was wrong, but how to make it right.

God is Near in Gentleness

Philippians 4:5 says, *"Let your gentleness be evident to all. The Lord is near."*

Gentleness isn't reserved only for those who "deserve" it. It is extended to everyone God created.

Emotional strain or stressful moments don't diminish the call to gentleness because God's gentleness toward us never wavers. Everyone has heavy days, hard moments, and hidden battles, and each one is still worthy of compassion, even when you feel like not giving any.

When a mother speaks with gentleness, heaven leans close. Her words become a conduit of comfort and conviction all at once.

Sometimes that nearness shows up in the smallest moments, like when a mother clenches her jaw to exhale before answering a defiant "no," or when she lowers her tone instead of matching theirs.

Those tiny pauses are where God's nearness fills the gap between emotion and grace.

Building Bridges Through Gentleness

Gentleness disarms defensiveness and builds bridges where anger would build walls.

It creates an atmosphere where repentance feels possible, where hearts stay open instead of hardened.

A gentle word can reopen doors that frustration slammed shut. It invites conversation instead of confrontation.

It gives a child permission to come closer instead of pulling away.

A Gentle Home Becomes a Safe Place

When a mother corrects with gentleness, her home becomes a refuge rather than a battlefield, a place where discipline leads to growth, not guilt.

She becomes a safe landing place for her children's hearts, the kind of mother they run to, not from. In this way, she mirrors Jesus, who is *"gentle and humble in heart". Matthew 11:29 (NIV)*

Gentleness is countercultural, yet deeply Christlike.

As the Fruitful Mom chooses calm over control, her home becomes a living illustration of God's compassion, firm in truth, soft in approach. Her children learn that real authority is not built through fear but through love that listens, corrects, and restores.

Being Gentle with Yourself

Gentleness is not only for how a mother treats her family; it's for how she treats herself.

When a Fruitful Mom fails, she does not condemn herself. She takes her thoughts inward, letting the Spirit refine them as she adjusts her steps.

Instead of escalating tension, she diffuses it. Instead of sharp replies, she answers softly, knowing that *"a gentle answer turns away wrath" Proverbs 15:1 (NIV)*, even when that gentle answer is for herself.

A Fruitful Mom's peace becomes persuasive, her calm contagious.

This fruit doesn't grow naturally; it grows through prayer, humility, and time. It's formed in those moments she wishes she had paused longer or spoken softer.

Battle Ready

It requires spiritual awareness, recognizing that the real battle isn't *"against flesh and blood". Ephesians 6:12 (NIV)*

The enemy seeks to divide through impatience, irritation, and misunderstanding.

But the Fruitful Mom resists with spiritual weapons like prayer, Scripture, and peace. She puts on the Armor of God and invites the Holy Spirit to rule where her flesh once reacted.

Over time, this transforms impulsive responses into intentional ones, turning potential conflict into opportunities for growth, making room for healing.

Through gentleness, a Fruitful Mom acknowledges that both children and adults need grace to grow. It reminds her to have the mind of Christ; to do as He would.

The Maturing Strength of Gentleness

Over time, her gentleness becomes the soft soil where her family's confidence grows.

It teaches her children that love and firmness can coexist; that discipline can still feel safe and truth can still sound kind. They learn that gentleness isn't the absence of power; it's the direction of it.

It's strength that knows when to speak, when to stay silent, and when to simply sit beside someone who's hurting.

Children grow up remembering that gentleness doesn't erase boundaries; it reinforces them with grace. It says, "I love you enough to correct you, and I'll love you through it too."

Grace and Strength Together

Gentleness teaches that grace and strength are not opposites; they are partners. The more a mother leans into grace, the stronger she becomes.

And the more she matures in strength, the softer her grace grows. It's the paradox of Christlikeness, to be bold in conviction yet tender in approach.

This balance allows her to raise children who are not just well-behaved, but well-loved. They will understand that kindness is not weakness, and humility is not fragility.

Gentleness as Prayer

Gentleness doesn't mean you never raise your voice; it means you raise your heart before your voice.

It's the prayer you utter before responding and the posture of humility that says, "Lord, let my words bring life, not harm."

Gentleness invites God into the conversation before your emotions do, transforming what could have been a moment of division into a moment of discipleship.

And from that steady balance of grace and strength grows the final fruit... one that anchors all the rest: **Self-Control**.

Because without self-control, gentleness cannot last. Self-control is what holds gentleness in place when emotions become overwhelming, when patience is thinned, and grace is tested.

Together, they form the quiet strength of a mother led by the Spirit; one whose peace cannot be provoked and whose love cannot be shaken.

Closing Reflection

Gentleness is strength surrendered to the Spirit. Let Him soften your responses and strengthen your heart. Trust that He is more than enough.

Personal Insight

Gentleness did not come naturally to me in every moment. There were times frustration spoke louder than grace. But God began teaching me that gentleness is strength that does not need to shout. It is Spirit-led.

The moments when I slowed my tone, softened my expression, and chose compassion over reaction became some of the most healing moments in my home.

Gentleness reminds me that hearts are tender, and God has trusted mine to steward others. Through His Spirit, I am learning that gentleness doesn't just shape my children. It also reshapes me.

Moments of Reflection

1. How can you speak truth in love this week with grace, and gentleness?

2. What can gentleness toward yourself look like after a difficult day?

3. How might your home change if gentleness became your first response?

4. In what ways do you see God's gentleness reflected in your own journey?

5. Is there a relationship, conversation, or situation in your life right now where God may be inviting you to respond with gentleness instead of reacting in frustration? How might surrendering that moment to Him change the outcome?

Prayer for Gentleness

Father,

Clothe my heart in gentleness. Let my words carry life, not weight. When tension rises and emotions pull strong, help me pause, breathe, and respond with grace instead of reaction.

Teach me to correct with compassion, to listen with patience, and to guide without wounding.

Let my voice be a place of safety for my children and peace for my home.

Remind me that gentleness is not weakness, but strength surrendered to You. Soften every harsh edge in me, heal every place where frustration has rooted, and make my spirit tender like Yours.

When I fall short, help me repent quickly and repair with humility. Let my children remember my actions through peace as a mother who loves deeply, leads in kindness, and treats them with the same grace You have poured over me.

Shape my heart to reflect Yours, so that they can better understand and know You.

In Jesus' name,

Amen.

Chapter Nine
SELF-CONTROL is the Heart's Guardian

A man without self-control is like
A city broken into and left without walls.

Proverbs 25:28

The Quiet Guard

Self-control is the quiet guardian of all the other Fruits of the Spirit.

It's what holds love steady when its tested, what keeps peace from unraveling under pressure, and what allows gentleness to stay gentle when emotions want to run wild.

Without self-control, the fruits spoil under pressure. With it, they flourish even in weathering times.

Let the Spirit Lead

For the Fruitful Mom, self-control isn't about suppression. It's about yielding to God's commandments.

It's not gritting your teeth and holding it together by sheer willpower; it's learning to restrain yourself long enough for God's Spirit to take the lead.

Self-control is impossible without the Word of God; because of this we can see how it works hand in hand with the Sword of the Spirit.

Scripture cuts through emotional impulses, intrusive thoughts, temptations, and reactive patterns. When a mother picks up this sword, she chooses clarity over chaos and truth over impulse.

Self-control becomes the fruit that takes the Word and uses it wisely: to pause before reacting, to silence lies with truth, to guide her emotions with Scripture, and to direct her desires toward God's will.

With the sword in hand, a mother becomes strong, steady, and spiritually disciplined.

Walls That Protect Peace

Proverbs 25:28 says, *"Like a city whose walls are broken through is a person who lacks self-control."*

Without boundaries of restraint, our emotions become open doors for negative influences to take control over our actions. But when a mother practices self-control, she builds strong walls of wisdom around her heart and home; not walls that keep people out, but walls that protect peace within.

When Self-Control Feels Impossible

There will be days when self-control feels impossible or even forgotten.

When the morning rush turns into a meltdown, the noise feels endless, and your patience feels like a thread about to split. You'll want to yell, slam a door, or walk away begrudgingly.

But self-control speaks, "Pause. Pray. Do what God says is right, then proceed."

This does not deny your feelings. It disciplines them. It reminds you that emotions are real, but they don't have to rule over your decisions and actions.

For example, when your toddler spills juice all over the freshly mopped floor, or your teenager talks back with an attitude.

The old you might react instantly. But, the Spirit-led you takes a moment to pause, looks them in the eye, and says calmly, "This is not appropriate behavior, but we can work on this together."

That moment doesn't just teach accountability. It teaches redemption.

That's the power of self-control: it transforms messes into lessons. It models the same grace God shows us when we make mistakes: patient, firm, and full of love.

Self-Control in Everyday Choices

It's walking away from gossip instead of adding to it. It's turning off a show that stirs what shouldn't be stirred. It's saying no to distractions that drain your spirit.

Sometimes it looks like biting your tongue when your family member speaks harshly, trusting that God can work on their heart better than your reaction ever could.

Other times it's choosing to stay off your phone at dinner, giving your children your full attention instead of divided affection. Self-control teaches your home that love is not impulsive. It's intentional.

It's the spiritual discipline that guards your heart and theirs from unnecessary wounds.

Most battles of self-control are won in the mind before they ever reach the mouth.

It's in the moment when thoughts start spiraling, "I can't do this, they don't appreciate me, this is too much," that the Fruitful Mom stops and redirects. She replaces those lies with truth:

"I can do all this through Him who gives me strength" Philippians 4:13 (NIV)

When she chooses to pause and pray instead of panic and speak, she gives the Holy Spirit time to rewrite the outcome. What could have become a memory of regret becomes a testimony of grace.

Every time she chooses calm over frenzy, she teaches her children that emotions are not the enemy. They're simply energy that needs direction and control.

Self-control is not a one-time achievement; it's a daily rhythm of reliance. It's the decision to wake up and say, "Holy Spirit, help me master my moments before they master me."

Some days you'll do well, and other days you'll miss the mark, but that's where grace meets growth.

When you raise your voice, self-control helps you lower it again. When you overreact, it helps you apologize without shame. When you feel like you've lost your patience completely, it gently reminds you that you can always start over.

The Fruitful Mom comprehends that every time she surrenders her reactions to God, she's not failing; she's forming. Her faith is being trained to respond from the Spirit rather than from stress.

Your Children Are Always Watching

Children rarely learn self-control through lectures; they learn it through observation.

They notice when you stay calm instead of blowing up. They notice when you walk away to pray instead of retaliating. They notice when you admit your mistake and say, "I shouldn't have spoken like that," or "I shouldn't have done that, forgive me."

One day, they'll mirror that same pattern in their own conflicts, pausing before they lash out, following God's way before they respond. That's the legacy of self-control: it teaches restraint through relationships.

Life's Testing Ground

Self-control is challenged most when a mother is tired, overwhelmed, or misunderstood.

It's easy to be composed when life feels calm, but true maturity shows when life feels chaotic:

- when you're running late, and someone cuts you off in traffic,

- when you've repeated yourself for the tenth time to your children and no one changes their behavior, and

- when you've poured out love and get silence in return.

These moments don't define your failure. They refine your faith.

Mothers need to make a conscious effort to realign their thoughts with what the Word says. It is a process, a slow shaping one, but one that becomes achievable with God by your side.

Every surrendered reaction strengthens your spirit. Every pause builds spiritual muscle.

The more you choose God's principles in every circumstance, the easier it becomes to recognize His voice in troubling situations. With practice, self-control becomes not just something you do, it becomes who you are.

Guarding the Gates

Proverbs 4:23 says, *"Above all else, guard your heart, for everything you do flows from it."* Self-control is the gatekeeper of that command.

It guards what enters your mind, what leaves your lips, and what settles in your spirit.

It keeps bitterness from taking root and grace from running dry. A mother's self-control doesn't just protect her peace; it preserves her influence.

Her children learn to trust her guidance because they see that her emotions don't drive her decisions; her faith does.

This is why I often remind my children that they cannot unsee what they've seen, nor unhear what they've heard. Every image, word, and sound that passes through their eyes and ears becomes a seed planted in their hearts.

As their mother, I have a God-given responsibility to guard those gates. That's why I place certain restrictions on what they watch on television, listen to in music, or scroll through on their devices.

These boundaries aren't made to hinder them, but to protect them; to preserve their innocence and shape their discernment. Their spiritual and moral character is far more valuable than momentary entertainment and social pressures.

And truthfully, this lesson isn't just for children. Even adults must learn to practice self-control, for what we continually allow to enter our minds will eventually shape what flows out of our hearts and mouths.

With God, the Fruitful Mom discerns that self-control is not about domination. It's about direction and confidence in Him.

It's not about holding everything together perfectly; it's about letting God hold you together faithfully. Because the One who is truly in control is the One who lives within you.

A Legacy Written in Love

In the end, being a Fruitful Mom isn't about always getting it right. It's about your intentions and discernment in Christ.

It's the daily decision to abide in Christ so His Spirit can bloom through you, turning ordinary moments into eternal seeds.

Every act of patience, every word of kindness, every pause of self-control becomes part of a living legacy written not on paper, but on hearts.

Your children may forget your words, but they will never forget your walk; the steady faith, the quiet strength, the love that reflected the heart of God.

Your fruit becomes your godly lineage. Your home becomes your garden. And your life becomes a reflection of John 15:8:

"This is to My Father's glory, that you bear much fruit, showing yourselves to be My disciples." (NIV)

For the Fruitful Mom, every day, no matter how messy, loud, or unseen, is an opportunity to glorify the Gardener who planted her. And as she abides in Him, she will continue to flourish... even through any storm.

Closing Reflection

The pause is powerful. Every moment you stop, breathe, and choose God's way is a victory of the Spirit within you.

Personal Insight

Self-control has felt like one of the most refining fruits. It's tested in stress, fatigue, and emotional moments when it would be easier to react than to respond.

But God has shown me that every pause, every prayer before speaking, every moment I surrender my impulses to Him becomes a victory of the Spirit within me. I am learning that self-control isn't about being in control, it's about yielding to God's purpose.

It's about letting God guide my responses so that my words and actions plant life instead of regret. And each time I surrender, He strengthens me.

Moments of Reflection

1. When was the last time you paused before reacting and how did that change the outcome?

2. What moments most test your self-control, and how might you invite God into them before they happen?

3. How can you model restraint for your children in ways they can see and understand?

4. What emotion or habit might God be asking you to surrender so His peace can guard your heart more fully?

5. How can you celebrate progress, not perfection, in your journey toward Spirit-led self-control?

Prayer for Self-Control

Lord,

Strengthen me to master my moments, and to not be mastered by them. When my emotions rise, let Your Spirit rise higher. When impatience tries to speak first, give me the wisdom to pause and the grace to respond with peace.

Help me guard my heart, my thoughts, and my tongue, so that my words build, not break. Teach me to recognize when I need to step back, breathe, and invite You into my reactions.

Remind me that self-control is not about perfection, but surrender. Remind me to let You lead before my feelings do. When I fall short, help me reset quickly, apologize humbly, and begin again with grace.

May my children learn restraint by watching me walk in Yours. Shape my habits, renew my mind, and steady my spirit, so my home is filled not with reaction, but with Your peace, patience, and love.

In Jesus' name,

Amen.

Chapter Ten
Bonus: When Fear & Faith Collide

The Valley No Mother Asks For

There are moments in motherhood when even the strongest self-control slips through trembling hands; moments when fear rises faster than you can steady your breath.

After walking through the fruits that shape our daily rhythms, we must pause in a different kind of place; the valley where fear and faith meet head-on. Every mother eventually reaches a moment she never expected to face when her child is hurting, threatened, or fighting for their life.

In these moments, motherhood becomes more than choices and responses; it becomes a collision of raw emotion and desperate trust in God. This chapter steps gently into that personal space, where a mother's greatest fear meets the God who holds her through it.

When a mother faces the possibility of losing her child through illness, injury, or unexpected complication, time seems to stop.

The world narrows to a single prayer: "Lord, please... not my child."

Fear tries to enter within her. Faith quivers, yet still reaches toward God. Both cling to the God who sees every outcome.

This chapter is for the mother holding on by a thread, praying through tears, and wondering if God truly hears her cry.

Faith in the Valley

There was a moment in my own journey when fear and faith collided so violently that I thought my heart would stop. It was the moment I realized I might lose my youngest child, my surprise baby, the one I was certain would look most like my husband.

Nothing prepared me for that kind of terror. Nothing steadied me except the desperate cry that rose from a place deeper than words. I didn't know then how the story would end, although I knew what I so desperately wanted in faith.

I knew that I was a mother facing the unthinkable, just like so many others. And it was in that valley that God met me.

My Story: When I Thought I Would Lose My Son

I remember the day my heart dropped, and concern flooded my entire body. I was pregnant with my youngest son when something shifted, and suddenly I knew something was wrong. The possibility of a miscarriage became real. Heavy. Immediate.

My family and I had gone on our first family cruise vacation to the Bahamas. We had just ported at one of the Islands for the night.

We were all excited and very hungry, and at that time I had four kids who were starving, so we went to a pizzeria at the hotel port.

There, we laughed, waited, and enjoyed a delicious pie of pizza. Then suddenly, I felt a warm trickle down below.

I somehow knew immediately what was going on... I was bleeding.

I quickly told my husband, "We need to leave and we need to leave right now." He saw the look on my face and without question, helped me gather the kids so we could leave in a hurry.

They were all trying to keep up with my fast pregnant walk. My husband finally asked with deep concern as he kept all the kids together, "What's wrong?"

I remember his face when I told him, "I'm bleeding."

He turned pale instantly, and he somehow made everyone walk even faster.

As soon as we arrived in the hotel room, he told me to go in the shower. I immediately requested him to call our pastors to pray for us.

I don't think my husband understood the gravity of the situation until he saw all the blood dripping out of my body.

I honestly do not know how he held everyone together while I stood bare in the shower, pouring out gushes of blood down the drain, and our children were outside in the next room.

I heard him making phone call after phone call, reaching out to every pastor and prayer warrior we knew. He called hotel management too.

I, on the other hand, was crying out to God for the life of my child.

Days prior, my pastor had shared a testimony with her congregation that became the stepping-stone I used to stay in faith during this devastating and heart wrenching experience.

She shared that she was once in a car accident with her children when they were younger. One of her kids was severely hurt, unconscious, and bleeding out of her mouth.

It was presumed she wasn't going to make it as she lay in the emergency room. But my pastor stood in faith and prayed to God in strength and certainty. Eventually, she received news that her daughter was alive and well.

No one knew why or where the blood came from. The little girl had no external or internal injuries. It was unexplainable and baffling to the doctors. They simply told my pastor that they didn't know where the blood came from... that it happens sometimes.

But she knew... it was God's hand that healed and answered those faithful and earnest prayers.

My pastor ended her testimony with, God is no respecter of persons. What He did for her; He can and will do it for you.

I held on to those words with every fiber of my existence, crying there in the shower practically kissing the cold tiles on the wall in front of me with every breath and word.

It felt like an eternity, but my pastor was finally on the phone and we all prayed together. She repeated and declared "God is no respecter of persons. What He did for me; He will do for Brenda."

After praying with her, my husband told me to get dressed. We were going to the ER.

Our four children could not come. We were forced and at the same time blessed to be able to leave them at the hotel. The manager came and took our kids to their kids' club, which they closed down to privately care for them.

Once the ambulance came and I was strapped into a chair, I thought all would be well...

But no...

Because I had showered and put on clean clothes, there was no outward evidence of bleeding. It did not look like I was in a serious state of emergency.

I held my legs tightly together, so no bleeding was visible.

This made them leave me in a hallway for what felt like hours. I also knew that there were some issues about payment. I was not seen until my husband was able to pay a few thousand dollars out of pocket.

Eventually, I was rolled into a room, told to change into a gown, and placed on a bed.

When the doctor came, he did not seem concerned or worried. Bear in mind, my legs were still tightly pressed together. It wasn't until he spread my legs apart that he jumped back, startled, and let out a gasp.

A huge gush of blood splattered everywhere. It fell on him, on the bed, and all over the floor.

Blood was everywhere.

It covered everything.

It literally looked like a massacre had taken place in that room.

My husband's face looked paler than I had ever seen it. He told me later that day that he had seen a fetus on the floor.

The doctor quickly called a nurse and had her clean up the area so he wouldn't slip. I was still praying and believing my child was alive and well.

Once he was able to examine me, he poked and prodded, very roughly. It felt as if, if my baby was alive, he might accidentally harm him further.

When he was done, he told us that he felt a hole in my uterus and that I lost the child. I did not accept this. I needed evidence. They were forced to ferry the sonographer from another island to confirm the status of my child at an additional cost to us.

Even though I was devastated to hear the doctor's words, I still held onto hope and faith that my son was not dead.

Once inside another room, the sonographer, who was not informed of the situation, prepped her tools and began searching.

As soon as she placed her ultrasound probe on my belly, my husband and I heard a heartbeat.

It was loud.

It was clear.

And it was immediately turned off by the doctor.

The sonographer was surprised and was pulled aside. I could hear the doctor's disbelief in the muffled background.

My husband and I smiled at each other with renewed hope. Tears of joy filled my eyes. I knew my child was alive.

The sonographer apologized and continued the scan in silence. She let us know she was not allowed to disclose any information until the doctor reviewed it.

She then sent us back to our room. I saw remnants of blood on the floor that had not been fully removed.

And it was in that room, the room where I had been told, "You miscarried," that the doctor returned and had to take back his words.

He looked confused as he handed me a sonogram photo of my healthy son. He didn't understand or know why this all happened.

He then repeated the same words the doctors told my pastor so long ago:

"We don't know where the blood came from" and then continued, "This happens sometimes."

But I knew exactly why my son was alive.

God did it.

God heard my cry, and in my story, He allowed me to keep my son,

not because my faith was perfect,

not because I prayed the "right" way,

not because I earned a miracle...

but because He is compassionate and near to His daughters in their distress.

I need you to understand something. I was not expecting twins. I had ultrasound photos taken in the past. I was only expecting one child. I cannot explain what my husband saw, but I do know God performed a miracle for our family that day.

But I must say this gently and honestly:

Not every mother receives the outcome she longs for.

And I share my story not as a comparison, but as a testimony of God's nearness, not His guarantees.

God was with me when I fought against losing my son.

And He is just as present with the mother whose story ends differently.

My miracle is not proof of stronger faith, and her loss is not proof of a weaker faith.

Both mothers are held by the same loving God who cares and carries them in His hands.

Why This Chapter Matters

This chapter was not planned. It was born out of a moment of urgent intercession for my friend's son, who at the time of completing this book, was fighting for healing in the ICU. *(Now fully recovered against all natural odds.)*

As I prayed for her and her son, I realized my book needed to hold space for the mothers who live in the valley where fear and faith collide; the mothers who must reach for the Fruits of the Spirit not from a place of calm routine, but from a place of trembling faith.

And then, the same day of this revelation, I received heart wrenching confirmation of this chapter's necessity when another dear friend, from college, lost her precious child days prior.

Two mothers. Two valleys. One hope-filled... one grief-stricken.

Their stories pressed this chapter into my spirit and reminded me that motherhood is not only about love, discipline, and daily strength.

It is also about the private, painful places where love must anchor us, where patience feels impossible, where peace must be fought for, where gentleness becomes a lifeline, where faithfulness keeps us standing, and where self-control means clinging to God instead of collapsing under fear.

Even here, especially here, the Fruitful Mom needs the Fruit of the Spirit.

And even here, God draws near when our hearts break.

A Mother Waiting in Hope

There is a particular ache reserved for the mother who is still waiting; the mother who sits in hospital rooms, pacing hallways, refreshing her phone, or lying awake praying for news that hasn't come yet.

The valley of "not knowing" or "fully expecting" can be its own kind of torment. It stretches time and weighs the heart, making every breath feel like a prayer and every minute feel like a battle.

If you are a mother in this place, hear this: any fear that may try to overwhelm you, does not disqualify your faith. Stand on God's Word and He will sustain you.

You can feel fear trying to seep in and still trust God. You can cry and still believe. You can shake and still stand.

Faith was never meant to remove your humanity; it was meant to lead you back into the arms of the One who created it.

God is near to you in this waiting. He sees the child you are pleading for. He sees the strength you don't feel you have.

And in this valley, the Fruitful Mom does not rely on her own strength; she leans into the Spirit who steadies her trembling heart.

And He is holding you even now. You are not alone. Pushing back fear even though it is extremely hard, does not make you weak... it makes you a mother.

And hear this, too: what God has done for me, He is fully able to do for you. He is still the God of miracles, still the God who hears, still the God who rescues and restores.

But even if your story does not unfold the same way mine did... even if the valley leads you somewhere you never wanted to go... your story is not over.

God is still faithful. There is still purpose after tragedy. There is still life, breath, meaning, and a future on the other side of the pain that tries to break you.

Hope is not tied to outcomes; it is tied to Him.

And He will carry you through every step of this valley, no matter how your story ends or has ended.

A Mother Grieving and The Unthinkable

There is no pain on Earth like the pain of a mother whose child is no longer here.

It is this heartbreak that changes the shape of a mother's world. It is a silence that echoes, a memory that burns, and a love that does not know where to go.

If this is your valley, hear this: your grief is holy; it's a testimony for others to draw strength from when ready.

Your love for your child is evidence of God's image within you; fierce, eternal, and deeply felt.

Your child mattered.

Your motherhood remains.

And God is near to the brokenhearted in ways deeper than language.

He weeps with you. He carries you. He holds what your heart cannot hold alone.

And in a valley like this, the Fruitful Mom does not reach for strength she does not have, but allows the Spirit to hold her with the fruits she cannot produce on her own:

Peace that steadies what is shattered, gentleness that softens what is raw, faithfulness that reminds her God has not left, and love that continues even when her arms feel unbearably empty.

These fruits do not erase the grief; they simply breathe with her through it... they are quiet, sacred companions in a valley no mother ever wanted to walk.

When We Ask, "Why My Child... and Not Theirs?"

One of the heaviest questions a mother will ever whisper is the one she rarely dares to say out loud:

"Why my child? Why is my child still here... while another mother is grieving?"

And for the grieving mother, the question aches just as deeply:

"Why is her child alive... while mine is gone? Why was her prayer answered with life... and mine with loss?"

There is no comparison sharp enough to hold this ache.

No mother earns a miracle. No mother deserves a loss.

The outcome does not reflect a mother's righteousness, nor does it reflect God's favoritism. We will carry the mystery of "why" until heaven, but we do not carry it alone.

And while God never asks a mother to understand the unthinkable, He does promise that no valley is wasted. He brings purpose out of what was meant to break us.

One mother's story may ignite hope, another mother's story may release strength, but both are carried, seen, and treasured by God. Their testimonies do not explain the "why," but they shine with the truth that God is still present in every story.

With time, healing will come, and peace will follow.

The Fruitful Mom will engulf herself in the Spirit in spite of emotional loss or gain, in every situation she never wanted to enter.

Love reminds her that both children mattered to God. Joy, though dim, promises that eternity is real and restoration is coming. Peace settles over the questions no human words can calm. Patience gives her grace for the long healing that grief demands.

Kindness helps her speak gently to herself as she wrestles with guilt and confusion. Goodness protects her from believing God is unfair or cruel. Faithfulness assures her that God did not leave her; not for one second. Gentleness softens the edges of her sorrow. Self-control helps her silence thoughts that blame her or compare her to other mothers.

These fruits do not remove the ache, but they give her the strength to walk with it.

God is present in both stories... in the miracle and the mourning.

He rejoices with one. He weeps with the other. And He holds both with the same unchanging love.

Closing Reflection

Every tear, every question, every breath taken in the valley is cradled in the hands of a God who does not let go. And the Fruitful Mom, even trembling, is never without His peace, His promise, or His everlasting love.

Personal Insight

There are valleys in motherhood no heart prepares for; places where faith is not loud and triumphant, but trembling and tear-stained.

Walking through this chapter, my heart is reminded that faith does not always look like certainty; sometimes it looks like breathing passed fear, whispering prayers when words feel fragile, and trusting God even when nothing makes sense.

I have learned that God's presence is not proven by outcomes, but by the way He holds us when we feel like collapsing under the weight of love and fear. In the miracle, He is near. In the loss, He is near. In the uncertainty, He is near.

This valley reminds me that being a mother does not mean being endlessly strong; it means being endlessly held. God does not measure us by how perfectly we stand, but by how willingly we lean on Him when we cannot.

Whether living in faith, waiting in aching silence, or grieving unspeakable loss, this truth remains: God is faithful, not only to the story, but to the mother living inside it. And even here, His love remains steady, gentle, and enough.

Moments of Reflection

1. Where in your own story have fear and faith collided, and how did you sense God drawing near to you in that moment?

2. Which Fruit of the Spirit do you feel yourself reaching for most in this season, and which one do you sense God inviting you to grow in as you walk through your current valley?

3. What unanswered questions, "the whys," or silent aches are you carrying today, and what would it look like to place them in God's hands, even without understanding the outcome?

4. How has God shown His faithfulness to you in past moments of fear, loss, or uncertainty, and how might remembering those moments strengthen you right now?

5. When you imagine placing your child, your fears, your grief, or your unanswered questions into God's hands, what part of your heart resists and what part quietly believes? How might God be gently inviting you to trust Him there?

Prayer for Mothers in Crisis

Father,

I lift every mother who is standing in the valley where fear and faith collide. You see the trembling in her hands, the heaviness in her chest, the prayer she is too exhausted to speak.

Draw near to her now. Let Your presence wrap around her like a gentle covering. Give her strength when she feels weak, peace when her heart races, and comfort when tears fall without warning.

Lord, for the mother who is waiting in faith or fear, steady her breath. Remind her that You are with her in every moment of uncertainty, holding what she cannot control. Be her refuge, her anchor, her quiet hope in the storm.

And for the mother who is grieving the loss of her precious child, hold her with a tenderness only You can give. Let her feel Your nearness in the ache she cannot explain.

Heal the wounds time cannot touch. Whisper to her heart that her child is safe in Your arms, and that You will walk with her through every moment of sorrow and every fragile step toward healing.

God, remind each mother that her tears are not unseen, her fears are not failures, and her pain is not ignored.

Uphold her with Your righteous right hand. Surround her with Your love. And let her know deeply, personally that You will never leave her, in this valley or in any season to come.

In Jesus' name,

Amen.

Chapter Eleven
Prayers & Reflections

The prayers and reflections in this section are provided as a supplement to the book, offering additional support when needed. They are not meant to replace personal prayer or time with God, but to serve as a gentle guide and encouragement.

Mothers may choose to use them fully, partially, or not at all, depending on the season they are in and the needs of their hearts. Each prayer is written to help focus faith, invite God's presence, and deepen reflection throughout the motherhood journey. These moments are meant to create space for stillness, honesty, and connection with the Lord.

Whether used in a quiet moment alone or revisited over time, they are designed to support spiritual growth without pressure or expectation. Use these reflections as an invitation to pause, breathe, and meet with the Lord in a way that feels natural, personal, and life-giving.

The righteous cry out, and
The Lord hears them;
He delivers them from all their troubles.
The Lord is close to the brokenhearted and
Saves those who are crushed in spirit.

Psalm 34:17-18

Prayer for the Fruit of Love

Heavenly Father,

Thank You for loving me with a love that is patient, unconditional, and unfailing.

I come before You asking that Your love would fill my heart in a deeper way.

Teach me to love the way You love; to be patient when I feel overwhelmed, gentle when I feel frustrated, and compassionate even when it feels hard to give.

Help me to see others the way You see them and to respond with kindness, grace, and tenderness.

Let Your love soften the places in me that have grown tired, guarded, or discouraged.

Lord, let Your love reshape my words, my thoughts, my reactions, and my attitude.

Help me love my family with intention and warmth, not out of obligation, but out of the overflow of Your Spirit in me.

When my strength runs low, remind me that Your love never runs out.

Root me in Your presence so deeply that love becomes my first response and not my last resort.

May Your love be the anchor of my heart and the atmosphere of my home.

In Jesus' name,

Amen.

Prayer for the Fruit of Joy

Heavenly Father,

Thank You that true joy comes from You and not from my circumstances.

I ask that Your Spirit fills my heart with a deep, unwavering joy; one that remains steady even in difficult moments.

Help me to remember that joy is not just a feeling, but a gift that grows when I trust You.

Teach me to see blessings in ordinary moments, to smile even through tears, and to rest in the assurance that You are always with me.

Let Your joy renew my strength, lift my spirit, and brighten my heart.

Lord, when life feels heavy or overwhelming, remind me that my hope is secure in You.

Replace discouragement with praise, frustration with gratitude, and weariness with renewed delight in Your presence.

Help me carry joy into my home, into my relationships, and into my day-to-day life so that others can see Your light through me.

May Your joy be my song, my strength, and my confidence.

In Jesus' name,

Amen.

Prayer for the Fruit of Peace

Heavenly Father,

Thank You for being the God of peace and for inviting me to rest in You.

I ask that Your Holy Spirit fill my heart and mind with a deep, steady peace that goes beyond my understanding.

Calm the worries that race through my thoughts, quiet the anxieties that weigh on my spirit, and help me release every burden into Your hands.

Teach me to breathe deeply, slow down, and remember that You are in control, working in ways I cannot always see.

Lord, let Your peace cover my home, my relationships, and every part of my life.

When chaos surrounds me, help me respond with gentleness instead of fear.

When uncertainty rises, anchor my heart in Your promises.

Fill my soul with stillness, confidence, and trust in You.

May Your peace protect my heart, steady my emotions, and guide my steps each day.

May Your peace prepare me for any battle that may come.

In Jesus' name,

Amen.

Prayer for the Fruit of Patience

Heavenly Father,

Thank You for Your patience with me; Your gentle grace that meets me every day.

I ask that Your Holy Spirit grow patience within my heart, especially when I feel stretched, hurried, or overwhelmed.

Help me slow down when everything in me wants to rush.

Teach me to pause before reacting, to listen before speaking, and to lean on Your strength instead of my own.

When things do not go as planned, remind me that You are still working, still present, still faithful, and in control.

Lord, help me extend patience to the people around me, especially those I love most.

Give me a calm spirit when frustration rises and a steady heart when challenges feel endless.

Let patience shape my tone, my words, and my responses so that I reflect Your love rather than my impatience.

May patience bring peace into my home, kindness into my relationships, and rest into my soul.

In Jesus' name,

Amen.

Prayer for the Fruit of Kindness

Heavenly Father,

Thank You for Your kindness toward me; kindness that is gentle, patient, and full of compassion.

I ask that Your Holy Spirit fill my heart so that kindness flows naturally from within me.

Help me slow down enough to see the needs of others, to speak words that heal instead of hurt, and to respond with tenderness even when I feel tired or overwhelmed.

Teach me to reflect Your heart, choosing grace over frustration, empathy over harshness, and love over indifference.

Lord, make kindness the atmosphere of my life and my home.

Let it shape my tone, my actions, and the way I treat every person You place in my path.

Help me be someone who comforts, encourages, and uplifts.

When my patience feels thin, remind me of how well You have treated me, reminding me to extend kindness to others.

May Your kindness shine through me in the little moments and the big ones, so that others see Your love at work.

In Jesus' name,

Amen.

Prayer for the Fruit of Goodness

Heavenly Father,

Thank You for Your goodness that never changes and never fails.

I ask that Your Holy Spirit shape my heart so that goodness grows within me; goodness that reflects Your character, honors You, and blesses those around me.

Help me desire what is right, pure, and pleasing to You, even when it's difficult or unseen.

Teach me to choose integrity when no one is watching and to walk in righteousness because I love You, not because I want to be noticed.

Lord, let Your goodness flow through my words, my actions, and the way I treat others.

Help me be a gentle example of Your love in my home and everywhere I go.

When my flesh wants to react or give up, remind me that goodness is powerful, healing, and deeply needed in this world.

Strengthen me to do what is right, to stand for what is true, and to live in a way that points others toward You.

May Your goodness shape my life and leave a testimony of Your presence in me.

In Jesus' name,

Amen.

Prayer for the Fruit of Faithfulness

Heavenly Father,

Thank You for Your unfailing faithfulness—constant, steady, and true in every season of my life.

I ask that Your Holy Spirit grow faithfulness within me so that my heart remains anchored in You.

Help me to stay committed to Your Word, consistent in prayer, and steadfast in trusting Your promises, even when I cannot see the outcome.

Remind me that You are always working, always present, and always faithful to complete what You begin.

Lord, help me reflect that same faithfulness in the roles You've entrusted to me.

Strengthen me to show up with love, to keep my word, and to remain devoted to the people and responsibilities You've placed in my care.

When I feel weary, renew my strength. When I feel discouraged, lift my spirit. When I feel uncertain, steady my heart.

May my life testify to Your goodness as I walk faithfully with You, day by day.

In Jesus' name,

Amen.

Prayer for the Fruit of Gentleness

Heavenly Father,

Thank You for the tenderness of Your heart and the gentle way You care for me.

I ask that Your Holy Spirit cultivate gentleness within me.

Help me slow my reactions, soften my words, and carry a calm spirit even in stressful or emotional moments.

Teach me to respond with compassion instead of frustration, to correct with love instead of harshness, and to treat others with the same care that You show to me. Let my tone, my presence, and my spirit bring comfort rather than tension.

Lord, make gentleness a strength in my life, not a weakness.

Help me to be steady when emotions rise, nurturing when others feel fragile, and humble when pride tries to take over.

Let gentleness shape the way I love my family, speak to my children, and engage with the world around me.

May my gentleness reflect Your heart, calming storms instead of stirring them, and pointing others to Your peace.

In Jesus' name,

Amen.

Prayer for the Fruit of Self-Control

Heavenly Father,

Thank You for giving me the strength and grace I need each day.

I ask that Your Holy Spirit develop self-control within me.

Help me pause before reacting, think before speaking, and choose wisdom instead of impulse.

Strengthen me when temptation rises, when emotions feel overwhelming, and when I am tempted to respond in ways that do not honor You.

Teach me to surrender my will to Yours so that my decisions, my words, and my actions reflect Your heart.

Lord, help me discipline my thoughts, my habits, and my responses so that I live with purpose and intention.

Give me the courage to say no to what harms my spirit and yes to what brings me closer to You.

When I feel weak, remind me that Your power is made perfect in my weakness.

Let self-control guard my relationships, nurture peace in my home, and guide me into a life that is pleasing to You.

In Jesus' name,

Amen.

A Prayer for Fruitful Moms

Heavenly Father,

We come before You with grateful hearts for the mothers who are walking faithfully and bearing fruit in this season.

Thank You for the quiet victories, the consistent obedience, and the love they pour out each day—often unseen, yet deeply known by You.

Lord, encourage their hearts. Remind them that their faithfulness matters, that the seeds they are planting are growing, even when the harvest is not immediately visible.

Strengthen them to continue doing good without growing weary, knowing that You are at work through every prayer, every act of love, and every moment of perseverance.

Cover them with Your peace. Let joy be renewed, hope be refreshed, and purpose be reaffirmed. Guard them from comparison and self-doubt, and help them rest in the truth that You have equipped them for this calling.

May they remain rooted in You, drawing strength from Your Word and guided by Your Spirit. Continue to shape their hearts, their homes, and their legacy for Your glory.

We thank You for the fruit already evident in their lives, and we trust You with what is still growing.

In Jesus' name,

Amen.

The Garden of Grace

Motherhood is not a race to perfection; it's a walk with the One who is perfect in love. It's learning, over time, that fruit doesn't grow from trying harder. It grows from resting deeper in God's presence.

Every moment of love, every act of patience, every pause of self-control is a seed planted in eternal soil. Some will bloom quickly, others will take time, but none are wasted when they are surrendered to the Gardener's hands.

The Fruitful Mom understands that her growth is not measured by comparison, but by connection. She is not defined by what she has lost, but by what God continues to redeem. Even the wilted places of her past can blossom again when touched by His grace.

The same hands that prune also protect. The same voice that corrects also calls gently, *"Abide in Me."* And as she does, her roots deepen in faith, her branches stretch in hope, and her fruit multiplies in love, feeding generations yet to come.

So, to every mother reading these words:

When you feel weary, return to the Vine.

When you feel unseen, remember the Gardener never stops tending to you.

When you fear you've failed, trust that He can still bring beauty from every broken place.

Your story is not over. Your fruit is still growing. And your garden, the one watered by tears, prayers, and faith, will one day overflow with grace.

"I am the vine; you are the branches. If you remain in Me and I in you, you will bear much fruit." John 15:5 (NIV)

A Mother's Reflection: Redemption in Bloom

Before you close this book, I want to share something deeply personal. Everything written on these pages has been lived before it was learned. The truths you've read were not born from theory, but from tears, mistakes, and the mercy of a patient God.

When I look back, I see places where I failed my children, not because I didn't love them, but because I didn't know how to be the mother I wanted to be. As I follower of Christ, I am consistently learning. God's heart and how to mirror it in my own home.

And sometimes, a person's best is not good enough... and... that's okay... God works with you wherever you are in your journey of motherhood as long as you're willing to let God work in you.

There were times I reacted when I should have listened, corrected when I should have comforted, and pushed when I should have prayed. Those moments still ache in my heart, not with shame, but with longing to do better.

To the mother who feels like she has failed... you are not alone. I have been there, standing in the quiet aftermath of regret, wondering if too much time has passed to make things right.

But God, in His grace, has shown me that it's never too late. It may take time. It may take humility. It may take many small steps toward rebuilding trust. But restoration is always possible with Him.

"I will repay you for the years the locusts have eaten" Joel 2:25 (NIV)

That promise isn't just for harvest fields; it's for hearts. God can restore the years spent in misunderstanding, immaturity, or misdirection. He can soften what was hardened and heal what was fractured by impatience, fear, or anger.

To my older children, if you ever read these words, please know my heart. I didn't know then what I know now. I was growing while trying to guide you. And though I fell short at times, my love for you never wavered. Every lesson I've learned, every truth I've written here, reflects my desire to do better in every aspect of my motherhood, to all my children.

And to every mother who sees her reflection in my story, remember this: repentance is not the end of your motherhood; it's the renewal of it. What you surrender to God, He can still use.

What was broken through ignorance can bloom again through wisdom. You are still growing fruit, even if some branches once withered.

The Fruitful Mom is not the one who gets it all right; she's the one who returns to the Gardener and says, "Lord, prune me again."

May your story, like mine, become one of redemption in bloom; proof that God still makes beauty from our becoming.

Prayer of Restoration

Heavenly Father,

Thank You for being patient with me; for loving me through every season of my motherhood, even the ones I wish I could rewrite. You have seen every tear I've cried, every mistake I've made, and every moment I've tried to do right but fell short. Yet You never turned away. You've only drawn me closer.

Lord, I bring before You the places I mishandled; the words I wish I had spoken differently, the silences that hurt, the times I chose control over compassion, and fear over faith. I ask for Your mercy to cover my failures and for Your grace to redeem what my hands could not fix.

Father, restore the bridges that time or misunderstanding has broken. Where distance has grown, plant connection. Where wounds still ache, pour healing. Where guilt has lingered, replace it with Your peace.

Teach me to love my children, all of them, the way You love me: patiently, truthfully, and without end. Help me see them through Your eyes, to speak life where there has been pain, and to be the steady reflection of Your gentleness in their lives.

And Lord, remind me that it is never too late: not for growth, not for forgiveness, not for grace. Let my story be a testimony that even what was once broken can bear fruit again under Your hand.

In Jesus' name,

Amen.

Prayer of Blessing for the Fruitful Mom

Heavenly Father,

I come before You with a grateful heart, asking for Your blessing upon my life as a mother. Help me become, and continue to be, a **Fruitful Mom**, one who reflects Your love, Your patience, and Your faithfulness in every season. Lord, fill me with Your Spirit so that the fruit of my life will overflow into my home. Give me love when I'm weary, joy when the days feel long, peace when my heart is stretched thin.

Grant me patience in the noise, kindness in the chaos, goodness in the unseen moments. Strengthen my faithfulness, my gentleness, and my self-control so that my children see Christ in me.

Teach me to sow seeds consistently, even when I feel it may not produce. Help me trust that nothing done in love is ever wasted. Let my words build, my hands bless, and my presence comfort.

Shape my heart to stay humble, steady, and surrender to You. Bless my home with Your presence.

Cover my children with Your protection. Guide them with Your wisdom. Grow them in Your truth. May they rise to live strong, godly lives that honor You.

Father, when I feel inadequate, remind me that Your grace is sufficient. When I am overwhelmed, whisper Your peace. When I question my impact, reassure me that You are working in ways I cannot see.

May I bear fruit in every season, not by striving, but by abiding in You. Make me a mom who plants with purpose, waters with prayer, and trusts You for the harvest.

I surrender my motherhood to You, and I receive Your strength, Your joy, and Your blessing today.

In Jesus' name,

Amen.

Acknowledgements

Primarily, I give all glory, honor, and praise to my Lord and Savior, Jesus Christ.

Every word on these pages exists because of His mercy, His patience, and His unfailing love.

He is the One who carried me through the valleys, refined me through the storms, and taught me that motherhood is not a task to survive, but a calling to embody His heart.

This book is a testimony of His faithfulness, and it belongs to Him.

To my mother, thank you for loving me through every season of my life. Your unconditional love is a steady place for me to land when life feels heavy, and your strength has always inspired me.

Thank you for showing me the kind of love that nurtures, forgives, and endures. I love you with all my heart and I have been blessed to have you as a mom.

To Pastor Brandi, thank you for being a spiritual anchor and faithful shepherd in my life. Your personal support, prayers, guidance, and example of godly womanhood have shaped me more than you know.

You are a true treasure and I will always stand with you if needed. You have poured into me, challenged me, and helped me see who I could become in Christ. Thank you for loving me, teaching me, and believing in me. I am forever grateful the Lord allowed our paths to meet.

To every mother reading this, whether you are in a season of joy, healing, rebuilding, or rediscovering who you are in Christ, thank you for turning these pages with an open heart.

My prayer is that you feel seen, strengthened, and reminded that you are not walking this calling alone. Heaven stands with you, and so do I.

May this book serve as a reminder that God uses ordinary moments to build eternal legacies.

About the Author

Brenda Lee Ginés is a Christian author, wife, mother, and homeschool educator who believes that faith is most powerfully formed within the rhythms of everyday family life. She writes to encourage mothers to grow spiritually not through pressure or perfection, but through abiding in God's presence.

As the founder of Faithistry Studios, Brenda creates devotionals and faith-based resources designed to help families see ordinary moments as sacred opportunities to walk with God. Her heart is to equip mothers to cultivate Christlike homes rooted in grace, truth, and the leading of the Holy Spirit.

Brenda's faith has been refined through both joy and deep adversity, including loss, illness, and seasons of rebuilding. Through every valley, she has witnessed God's restoring power—turning pain into purpose and strengthening her dependence on Him. These experiences shape the compassionate, hope-filled voice found throughout her writing.

She serves faithfully in her local church and is a Christian Mental Health Coach, combining biblical wisdom with gentle care to support emotional and spiritual healing. Brenda holds degrees in English Education and Christian Creative Writing, which complements her calling to teach, write, and disciple through words grounded in Scripture and lived faith.

Brenda believes faith, family, and creativity shape both her life and ministry.

Learn more about Brenda's books and resources at www.Faithistry.com.